I0632553

Brownlow Maitland

Theism or Agnosticism

An Essay on the Grounds of Belief in God

Brownlow Maitland

Theism or Agnosticism
An Essay on the Grounds of Belief in God

ISBN/EAN: 9783743423114

Manufactured in Europe, USA, Canada, Australia, Japa

Cover: Foto ©Lupo / pixelio.de

Manufactured and distributed by brebook publishing software (www.brebook.com)

Brownlow Maitland

Theism or Agnosticism

THEISM OR AGNOSTICISM:

AN ESSAY

ON

THE GROUNDS OF BELIEF IN GOD.

BY THE

REV. BROWNLOW MAITLAND,

AUTHOR OF "THE ARGUMENT FROM PROPHECY," "SCEPTICISM
AND FAITH," ETC.

LONDON:

THE CHRISTIAN EVIDENCE COMMITTEE OF THE
SOCIETY, FOR PROMOTING CHRISTIAN KNOWLEDGE;
NORTHUMBERLAND AVENUE, CHARING CROSS, W.C.;
43, QUEEN VICTORIA STREET, E.C.;
26, ST. GEORGE'S PLACE, HYDE PARK CORNER, S.W.
BRIGHTON: 135, NORTH STREET.
1886.

PREFACE.

THE author desires to introduce the following Essay to the reader with two explanatory statements respecting its method and plan.

1. The method followed throughout is the method of Consciousness, as distinguished from that of Logic; and the steps by which the theistic conclusion is reached are these.

Through direct consciousness of himself man discovers that he is possessed of a permanent Personality, endowed with Will, Intelligence, Moral and Spiritual Affections.

Through consciousness developed by observation and experience he learns that he is surrounded by an external Universe, and related to fellow-men of a like personality to his own.

Through consciousness further developed by reflection on himself and the Universe, he attains the conviction that over all is a Supreme

Personality, endowed with omnipotent Will, infinite Intelligence, perfect Righteousness and Love.

It is contended that these results of consciousness rest on the same basis, and stand or fall together. If the primary consciousness of a human Self is denied, all the rest vanish with it. On the other hand, if it is accepted, it carries all the rest in its train.

Thus it is from the knowledge of himself that man rises to the knowledge of God. Theism is the fruit of belief in man's real humanity; Agnosticism, of a virtual denial of his humanity.

2. As to the plan of the Essay, it has been thought best to present the subject in a continuous, unbroken discussion, without interruption from notes, references, or quotations from other books. To make it short, plain, and interesting to the general reader has been the aim, and to promote this aim the plan adopted has appeared to be the most suitable.

The author is sensible, however, of one disadvantage attending it, inasmuch as it deprives him of the pleasure of acknowledging his debt to many who have preceded him in the same field of inquiry. The literature of the subject is so extensive, that every one who adds to it must owe much, consciously or unconsciously, to the labours of his predecessors. He hopes that this general acknowledgment will be accepted as sufficient; but for his own satisfaction he cannot refrain from expressing his obligation to one singularly suggestive work, " *The Philosophy of Natural Theology*," published in 1874, by the Rev. William Jackson, the Bampton Lecturer for the following year.

CONTENTS.

THEISM OR AGNOSTICISM;

AN ESSAY ON THE GROUNDS OF BELIEF IN GOD.

—◆—

CHAPTER I.

THE SUPREMACY AND FRUITFULNESS OF BELIEF IN GOD.

" I believe in God the Father Almighty."
Thus few and simple are the words which
express the fundamental article of the faith of
Christendom. But simple and few as they are,
there can be no doubt that the conviction to
which they give utterance is one of unequalled
import, and in any classification of convictions
with respect either to the magnitude of their
subject-matter, or their fruitfulness in the spheres
both of thought and conduct, would deserve to
stand first and to occupy a class by itself. Other
convictions or beliefs which take root in the

B

logical demonstration, than Art can be dealt
with by the carpenter's rule, or Morality by the
science of number.

Nor is it only in the way of widening the
method to be followed, and the field from which
evidence is to be sought, that our inquiry will
be affected by the unique vastness and fruitfulness of the idea of God. For as we pursue our
investigation, keeping ever present to our minds
the supreme character of the idea, it may be that
the very fact of its supremacy may go some way
towards impressing us with a conviction of its
truth. The appeal made by it to that instinctive
longing after a divine fellowship, which in our
best moments springs up out of the mysterious
depths of our personality, will exert a persuasive
force upon us; and the more we perceive how
wonderfully the idea of God answers to the wants
of our nature, and how perfectly it is adapted to
reinforce every influence which purifies the affections, invigorates the sense of duty, and endows
the soul with fortitude and hope, the more insuperable will be the difficulty of dismissing it
as a baseless dream, and the more will it attract
to itself our faith and trust.

It is true, indeed, that a practical conviction
of this kind may not be able to justify itself
formally in the eyes of the mere logician, but at

the bar of the higher reason it will be vindicated on the surer ground of experience. To the practical judgment of mankind the experience of supreme fitness, and of inexhaustible fertility in the production of beneficial results, is in general far more convincing than the formal demonstrations of argument; and from that judgment, at least in the moral and spiritual domain, there is no appeal. If thoughtful and earnest men come to feel that the idea of God is in harmony with all the higher aspirations and instincts of their nature, and exerts over the whole of human life an ennobling and cleansing influence, they will hold to the idea as substantially verified, and make little account of any theoretical objections which may be urged against it, or any deficiencies that logical subtlety may discover in the structure of the arguments employed in its vindication.

In claiming for this supreme belief a method of treatment and a range of evidence proportioned to its comprehensiveness, we are only applying to it a principle which governs the discussion of every question involving the social, moral, or religious elements of man's complex nature. Such questions cannot be determined by short and easy methods. They spread themselves over large spaces of human life, and must

be viewed in relation both to the higher consciousness and the practical needs of mankind.
Human nature is far too wonderful and mysterious to be subordinated to the rules of logic,
or explored by the methods of physical science.
It is unique in our world. If it is rooted in the
soil of material and animal existence, it towers
aloft into the purer atmosphere of spirit and
truth, of duty and religion. To that higher
region must all the questions of faith and conduct be carried, and there must the solutions of
them be sought. It is not open to us to dispose
conclusively of this or that proffered solution by
urging that a rigorous demonstration of it is
impossible. We hold and act upon a thousand
beliefs of which no formal demonstration can be
drawn out, and should justly deem it a mark of
insanity to pursue a contrary course. What we
really want to know about a practical belief in
the domain of morals or religion is, not whether
it can be proved true by processes of unanswerable reasoning, but whether it is in agreement
with our intuitions, our consciousness, our sense
of fitness and right; whether it gives satisfaction to the intellect, and repose to the heart;
whether it works well, in bringing harmony,
elevation, and nobleness into our lives. When
these are found by experience to be its qualities,

it asserts its own truth irresistibly, and reason, convinced and satisfied, demands no further proof.

In this view of the proper method to be followed in our inquiry there is, indeed, one obvious and momentous assumption, without which it would be untenable, — the assumption of our Humanity. Were this denied, to discuss questions of truth, morality, or religion would be absolute waste of time. To a creature which is nothing but a material organism, or animated automaton, without personality, will, moral consciousness, or spiritual intuition, such questions have no meaning and bear no relation. Call our higher nature by what name we will, mind or reason, soul or spirit, we must believe in it, and in its superiority to matter and animal existence, before it is possible for us to make a single step towards believing in eternal truth and goodness. It is only from ourselves that we can rise to God. If our consciousness of personality and will, our intuitions of right and duty, our aspirations after purity and truth, are thrust aside as untrustworthy and illusive, there will remain absolutely nothing wherein the belief in God can root itself within us. The universe might throb and glow with His presence throughout all its provinces, but we should remain unconscious of Him.

At the basis, then, of our inquiry lies the assumption that man is *human;* that is, a Person, endowed with reason, will, moral and spiritual affections, whose consciousness of mysterious superiority to the physical world and its organisms represents a real and ultimate fact of Being. With any one who refuses to admit this assumption, and denies the witness borne by his consciousness to his possession of human personality and reason, we do not pretend to argue.

We have spoken of belief in God as being supreme among beliefs, and of its consequences as affecting in a sovereign degree every province of human thought, emotion, and conduct. But it is only by drawing out this general statement into particulars, and tracing in detail the influences of the belief, that an adequate impression of its amazing fertility and power can be obtained. This therefore we will briefly attempt in these preliminary remarks, that we may carry with us into the ensuing discussion a sense of the infinite grandeur and inexhaustible fruitfulness of the idea, the truth and reality of which we are about to investigate.

What we have to picture to our thoughts is the theist, thoroughly penetrated and possessed by faith in God, the almighty, universal Father.

How will this faith mould his conceptions and influence his life?

Around him lies the physical universe, and on every part of it he will discern the impress of God. In the glories of the sky, and the wonders of the earth; in the countless varieties of vegetable and animal life; in every spectacle ef natural beauty, and every provision for human use; he will recognize the power, the wisdom, and the goodness of the Creator. Not a star that gems the night, not a flower that adorns the soil, not a fruit that affords nutriment for living things, will fail to whisper to him of God. The seasons as they run their beneficent round, bringing forth storm and calm, rain and sunshine, winter frosts and summer heats, and ripening the harvests for the sustenance of all living creatures, will be eloquent to him of a divine order; the solid earth with its mountains and valleys and garniture of green, the great oceans with their solemn swell and voice, the stately rivers and leaping streams, will testify to him of the Almighty Architect, whose mind conceived and whose hand built up the majestic structure of our globe. Standing in the midst of the glorious universe of visible being, and ranging with devout eye over its manifold phenomena, he will feel it to be a temple filled by

the omnipresent Deity, and from his heart will
ascend worship and praise unto Him who was,
and is, and is to come, of whom and for whom
are all these things.

But in this world of God's workmanship he
dwells not alone. He is one of a race, the successive generations of which during thousands
of years have lived and laboured, and then
passed away. How will he conceive of these his
fellow-men, as he looks back on the troublous
story of the Past, or sees the billowy sea of
Humanity heaving tempestuously around him?
Not as creatures of the dust, animated organisms evolved out of the ceaseless play of the elements by some blind Fate or unconscious Force;
but as children of a heavenly Father, and brethren to each other by virtue of their common
possession of a nature endowed with capacities
for truth and goodness. History, to the theist,
is instinct with a divine providence. He is confident that the destinies of mankind are held
within the grasp of infinite wisdom and love,
and that never, throughout its devious and
stormy course, has humanity been left without
the care and guidance of God. In this conviction of a divine Fatherhood he lives and
works and hopes for his race, and even in the
darkest hour of its fortunes he cannot despair,

for over all is the eternal Goodness and Truth.

Thus, to the believer in God, everything which lies outside his own personality, and is conceived of in his consciousness as being other than himself, is pervaded by a divine presence, and impressed with a divine purpose. Nothing is only what it is in itself; it bears the stamp of an originating Mind, and is irradiated by the glory of an eternal Beneficence. No iron chain of necessity binds together Past and Present and Future, but a holy Will which ordains and guides the course of the ages with a perfect prescience and wisdom. In a word, by belief in God the universe is transfigured; a light which is not its own shines through all its heights and depths, the light of Intelligence and Love; God is in all things, and all things are in God.

But what of the theist's own Self, that mysterious personality of which he is conscious, fraught with the burden of human affections and hopes? Will this be unaffected by the conviction of God's unceasing presence and activity? Can he feel, as he must have felt without God, an inexplicable, isolated, aimless unit of a soulless world? Impossible! Here, in the depths of his own being, will the presence of God be most vividly experienced, and relation to God

most comprehensively realized. In God he will
consciously live and move and have his being.
He will know God as his God, the Life of his
life, the Soul of his soul, more intimately connected with him than the nearest of his fellow-
creatures, the Source whence his being issues,
the Centre round whom it revolves, the End to
which it tends. And this sense of God, with
him and within him, will be the inspiring and
sustaining impulse of his affections and activities.
As the child of the heavenly Parent to whom all
things belong, he will walk amidst Nature and
encounter events with a strength and fortitude
which can spring from the conviction alone of
this filial relation; for him life will be charged
with a high and solemn responsibility,and in hope
and thankfulness will he daily present himself a
living sacrifice to the eternal Father and Lord.

But we must descend more into particulars
to estimate the full effect on his life of his
belief in God.

The lot of mortal man is a chequered one, and
the fountains of sorrow lie close by the springs
of gladness. Duty is often hard, and the will is
tempted to turn aside into easier ways; the
lower passions are imperious, and claim a sovereignty which belongs of right to the God-like
reason, reigning by the ministry of conscience

over the soul's activities and desires. Disappointment and decay cast their sombre shadows across every human path, and from the closing scene there is no escape. Thus life to the eye of sense is a medley, a struggle, an enigma, with a catastrophe ever impending over it, and nothing in it certain but death.

Into this perplexing scene the theist carries with him the belief in an almighty, ever-present Father, ordering his lot for him in wisdom and love. And lo! at the touch of this faith the scene is transfigured. Light breaks out in its dark places; its disorders and contradictions are comprehended within a higher harmony; the wavering will is reinforced with moral strength and vigour; sorrows are transmuted by a spiritual alchemy into the instruments of holy discipline and growth; death becomes the gate of life. All this change, this glorification of our dark and weary mortality, flows from the recognition of the divine Personality, as present and active in every phase and turn of human experience.

For to the theist sorrow and joy, prosperity and adversity, come from the throne of God. No blind forces deal them out to him mechanically, but a loving Hand mingles and apportions them. When days are bright, he not only enjoys, but is grateful; the sweet incense of thankfulness ascends from his heart to the Giver of all good, and the sense of a fatherly love comes down in return to hallow each innocent pleasure, and invest even the commonest blessings with a spiritual significance and grace. And when the wheel turns, and clouds darken his sky, it is not as if he were left to battle without sympathy or help against some remorseless power; he knows the Hand which chastens, and can bear with patience and hope, for sorrow as well as joy is God's minister to him for good.

Most of all in his moral conflicts will he experience the efficacy of his belief in God. For here he knows but too well his own weakness. Duty as a cold, impersonal law is not attractive. It commands, but neither persuades nor assists. The conscience confesses the obligation to obey, but too often the heart throws back a defiant refusal, or, at least, allows passion to overbear it, and temptation to betray it to evil. There is little prospect of the life becoming steadfastly righteous and noble, so long as duty is regarded as nothing more than a rule of utility, and conscience than a function of our material organism, or an instinct of our physical life. But let duty be identified with the will of God, and it starts into life and reality. Obedience to a

loving Father is a very different thing from
obedience to an impersonal law.   The greatness, the holiness, the goodness of God bear in
on the heart with an incalculable power,   and
with a mingled constraint and attraction draw
it to the side of virtue.   In every turn of the
moral conflict He is felt to be near, a personal
Presence of infinite purity and goodness, drawing
to Himself, sympathizing with and helping, the
soul which He made in His own likeness, and
longs to redeem and save.   No longer is man
in his sore struggle with temptation thrown
back merely on himself, and left to rely on his
own weak sense of self-respect for the force to
repel the onset of unworthy passions.   By a
vision of perfect purity and love he is arrested
and entranced, and rises to victory with the cry,
" How can I renounce and defy my Father and
my God ? "

Much more to the same effect might be added,
in illustration of the transcendent influence of
belief in God over every province of human
thought and conduct.   But it will be enough
for our purpose if we set over against the theist,
as thus imperfectly depicted, the portraiture of
one who looks out on the universe with an equal
intelligence, and feels within himself a like
instinct of morality, but knows nothing of God.

Man left by himself face to face with Nature is what we have to imagine. Man here, Nature there; that is all. A universe soulless, unconscious, blind; coming he knows not whence; sustained he knows not how; meaning he knows not what; hastening he knows not whither: and himself a conscious, thinking, suffering atom, coming into existence like a bubble tossed up on the time-stream, swept along by the play of unintelligent forces, and awaiting extinction by their unconscious agency at a date which cannot be distant. Truly an infinite enigma, and his own being the darkest part of it! For this consciousness, these human affections, this reason, which stir and energize within him, are apparently without any adequate source in which they originated, or any worthy purpose for which they exist. Out of the dust they seem to arise, and into the dust to vanish; illusive phantoms, gliding for a brief moment through the gloom, and melting away into nothingness.

What now has become of the glory of the universe, as the offspring and vesture of an infinite Mind, the witness of a supreme Beneficence, the minister of high purposes, the scene of discipline and instrument of blessing to innumerable children of immortality? Gone, all gone, for ever! for where there is no mind there can be no will, no purpose, no goodness; and the universe, bereft of the originating, indwelling, directing Deity, sinks into a senseless machine, impelled by some inexplicable necessity to produce and destroy, capable of no sympathy, and worthy of no gratitude.

And how fares man, alone with this unsympathizing, remorseless, fate-driven, godless universe? The higher his aspirations the vainer, for the doom of irremediable disappointment awaits them. To no purpose do the irrepressible instincts of his soul cry out for communion with the unseen and spiritual; above him he knows no mind to answer to his own, no God to whom his worship may ascend, no Father in whom his affections can find repose. Hope dies within his breast, for he has no future. Conscience becomes but a voice crying in the wilderness, for why should he toil and suffer for right, when right and wrong are but dreams of a day? " Let us eat and drink for to-morrow we die! "

With this contrast, however feebly drawn, before us we may surely assert with confidence, not only the amazing power and fruitfulness of belief in God, within all the departments of human thought and conduct, but also its singularly elevating character. Its whole unrivalled force goes manifestly to the development of man

c

in the highest line of culture which is possible
for him, and makes for the lifting him up in
the scale of existence, surrounding him with
witnesses to his spiritual relationship, and stir-
ring into energetic action all the higher faculties
of his being. And conversely it seems to be
equally manifest, that to be without faith in God
is to be destitute of the grandest idea which can
enlarge and ennoble the mind, and of the most
powerful motive which can uphold the moral
faculty, and enthrone it in its rightful sovereignty
over all the energies and passions of our nature.

Indeed, it is difficult to find words strong
enough to express adequately the practical difference between theism and atheism, in regard
to their full and ultimate effects on man's life
and thought. The theist and the atheist may
be said to live in different worlds; the one bask-
ing in everlasting sunshine, the light of mind
and purpose and love; the other wrapped in a
gloom through which no ray can pierce, the
darkness of physical, purposeless, inexplicable
necessity. And as their worlds are different, so
are even the personalities of which they are conscious in themselves. For the theist, recog-
nizing his place in a divine order, and his kindred
with the infinite Spirit, feels within himself a
real life derived from and upheld by the eternal,

self-existent Life, and knows his own personality to stand in permanent relation to the divine Personality in whom it exists. But the atheist, perceiving nothing but matter to which he can be akin, is constrained to conceive of his personality as of some transient sensation, secreted it may be of brain or gland, varying with each physical change, here to-day and nowhere to-morrow. Which of the two, the believer in God, or the unbeliever, is in the position that most conduces to dignity and progress, and is most likely to be fruitful of serenity and hope, every one can easily decide for himself.

When, therefore, we seriously consider all which belief in God is capable of doing for mankind, when allowed to inspire the soul and regulate the life, can we as rational beings help wishing and hoping that it may turn out to be founded on truth? Must it not be with a lively concern that we contemplate the possibility of its being torn from us by the advance of knowledge, and consigned to the limbo of poetic or superstitious fancies? Surely we should be less than men did we not cling to this supreme belief as long as possible, hope even against hope in its truth, and part from it, if part we must, with a poignant sorrow and bitterness of soul!

CHAPTER II.

THE EXISTENCE OF GOD NOT DEMONSTRABLE.

HAVING got before our minds the inherent
grandeur and momentousness of belief in God, we
now approach the great question, Is the belief
true? Can it be justified at the bar of reason?
That over the mind in which it unfolds
itself in its full magnitude and import it of
necessity exercises a sovereign rule, dominating
thought and conduct alike in all their provinces,
seems unquestionable; and in the conceptions
of such a mind it certainly invests the universe
with a purpose and a glory, and human nature
with a dignity and an aim, which on no other
supposition can be imagined possible. But
what substance, what reality, does it possess?
Must we sternly pronounce it to be, after all, a
mere dream, beautiful but baseless; a romance
constructed out of human aspirations and
desires, the poetry of the imaginative and restless soul? Or is there a solid external basis on

which it rests? Is man's conception of God a true and trustworthy intuition of a divine reality?

A tremendous question truly, before which every other is dwarfed into comparative insignificance! To discuss it with less than the utmost seriousness would be unworthy of a rational being.

Let us pause for a moment to inquire on which side the burden of proof may fairly be considered to lie. Naturally, one would at first reply, on the side of the theist. He asserts the fact of God's existence, and therefore is bound to furnish proof of his assertion; the practical atheist asserts nothing but his own ignorance, and waits to be convinced if possible. No doubt this would be a just and complete assignment of the burden of proof, if atheism had been in general possession of the field of thought, and theism were some novel theory started by individual minds to displace the old and universal opinion. But the real position of the antagonistic views towards each other is exactly the reverse. Theism has been in general possession of the world; it is atheism which is the exceptional opinion, propounded here and there by individual minds to bring about a revolution in the established belief of mankind. This undoubtedly in some measure shifts the burden of proof. A belief which antedates historical records, and in some form or other has reigned almost universally over human minds, and has been identified with almost all that has been most elevated in thought and most virtuous in practice, among all races and tribes of humanity, has on its side a fair presumption of its truth. Its antiquity, its universality, its peculiar power of rooting itself in the noblest part of human nature, and allying itself with man's best endeavours to advance in civilization and moral culture, give it a prestige which must be allowed considerable weight in the controversy respecting its truth. Whoever undertakes to assail it ought to produce solid reasons for attacking what almost all men have always believed and still believe, and the wisest and best men most of all. It is his procedure that needs to be justified. Those who have the mass of their fellow-men at their back may be satisfied with pointing to the mass as the justification of the common faith, until very cogent reasons are adduced to prove that faith erroneous. Thus the burden of proof is in some measure shifted to the atheist, who takes on himself to dispute and deny the most ancient and universal belief of his race.

It is true that in debates which can be conducted with logical precision, and concluded by

strict trains of unanswerable ratiocination, it is
of very little consequence on which side the burden of proof is considered to rest. Whether he
who affirms is required to make good his affirmation, or he who denies to substantiate his
denial, the argument moves on to an inevitable
conclusion, and the matter is placed beyond
all further controversy. But the practical
questions which concern human life and conduct do not belong to the class in which
absolute demonstration is possible. In these
there are moral probabilities on both sides to be
calculated, and reasons to be balanced against
each other which to different minds have
different degrees of force; and all such questions
run back more or less into those ultimate intuitions and instincts of our nature, of which
no logical account can be given, and no exact
estimate be made. Here it may often be of
considerable importance to determine where the
burden of proof lies. The reasons which might
be urged to justify the introduction of some
novel belief or practice, contrary to the general
opinions or habits of mankind, would need to be
greatly preponderant over those which could be
marshalled on the other side. Greater forces
are needed for the attack than for the defence.
It is the innovator who must prove his case

before he can expect to be listened to. Those
who have tradition and authority in their favour
need not be disturbed so long as a very decisive
case is not made out against them. They have
general consent on their side, and may challenge
their opponents to dislodge them from their
intrenchments, if they can.

The assailant of theism is therefore under
the disadvantage of being bound to take the
initiative, and bring forward a sufficient array
of reasons to persuade mankind to surrender the
grandest and most venerable of their beliefs. It
would not be sufficient for him even to show
that as much might be said against it as on its
behalf. Unless he can do more, his undertaking
will be practically a failure.

But having reminded him of this, we are
ready to listen to all that he can allege. And
what he says amounts to this, that the evidence
on which the belief in God has been supposed to
rest securely breaks down under modern critical
examination, and the idea of God is left floating
without support in the air, a mere figment of
the imagination to which there is no solid reason
for thinking that any external and independent
reality corresponds. This is the position taken
up by modern atheism, or agnosticism as it is
now called, to signify its negative character.

We know nothing about God, and can know nothing; His existence is incapable of proof.

Now when a proposition is said to be incapable of proof, it is important to ascertain what sort of proof the objector has in his mind. He may possibly be contemplating only some particular kind of proof, and that a kind which is not pertinent to the subject; and for the matter in question to be incapable of that would be no discredit to its claim to be considered true on other grounds. A Greek statue is certainly more beautiful than an African idol, but it cannot be proved to be so by the methods whether of mathematics or ethics or logic. Goodness and truth undoubtedly possess an intrinsic superiority to falsehood and vice; but the conclusion is not to be deduced from the maxims of political economy. The genuineness of affection cannot be proved by syllogisms, nor the possession of genius be ascertained by anatomical science. In all cases the test of truth and reality must be suitable to the nature of the thing to be examined, and a proposition is not to be pronounced baseless because there are methods of investigation and kinds of evidence which are powerless to establish its truth.

The proposition of the theist is that an eternal Mind or Spirit exists, of infinite power, wisdom, and goodness, in whom and by whom we and all things are. Our present question is, Supposing this were true, of what sort of proof might we deem it capable?

The agnostic replies, "Try every conceivable kind, and you will find every kind in turn to fail. You cannot discern God by the senses. You cannot find Him by scientific physical research. You cannot prove His existence by trains of abstract reasoning. You cannot arrive at Him by logical induction from the phenomena of the universe. What other possible mode can you suggest?"

The challenge seems formidable, but we do not shrink from accepting it. We confess that all those methods fail, and must fail, to demonstrate the being of God. But our contention is that they fail, not because God cannot be found by man, but because those methods are, by their very nature, inapplicable to the search for Him. And this we now proceed to show, by briefly examining the nature of these methods in succession, and pointing out how it is that they fall short.

First, the existence of God, even if it were the most certain and transcendent of facts, would certainly not admit of proof by evidence addressed to our bodily organs of sense. They have no relation to spirit, no capacity for perceiving anything but the presence and movement of what we call matter. The minds of our fellow-men are invisible, inaudible, intangible, to us; much more must be the Infinite Mind, even though it were not far from every one of us. Our senses can only make us conscious of material phenomena, and no material phenomenon can reveal its own cause or meaning. We might be startled by seeing the words, "There is a God," blazing across the midnight sky, or hearing the assertion pealed forth in awful thunders beneath the silent stars; but of itself the occurrence would prove nothing about God. The senses would perceive a sight or a sound; but neither sight nor sound would be God.

Nor would it be at all more possible to ascertain the existence of God by any of the processes of physical investigation. Far-reaching and subtle as these now are, they deal exclusively with material phenomena, and make their report to the bodily senses alone. They can never penetrate beyond the physical domain, never make us sensible of the presence of mind or spirit. To say, then, that no patient sweeping of the heavens with the telescope, no minute analysis of the composition of material substances, no searching for concealed forces

by the most finely balanced and sensitive
mechanisms, has ever revealed a trace of God,
is to say absolutely nothing to the purpose.
He might be filling all things with the might
of His presence and the splendour of His glory,
and yet it is certain that by no scientific
instruments could He be made apparent to us.

Failing to find God by the report of our senses,
or the processes of physical science, we might
try the method of abstract reasoning, and endeavour to discover Him at the end of a chain of
propositions, to each of which in turn the mind
could not refuse its assent. But a little consideration will make it clear that this method
also is inapplicable to the matter in hand.

Demonstrative reasoning, if the result is to
be accepted as certain, must have some indisputable basis to rest upon ; some truth or axiom
or fact from which it starts, and the consequences
of which it draws out and makes apparent. Such
a basis or starting-point, in order to be sure and
beyond all question, must be sought within our
own minds, in some ultimate conviction of which
we cannot rid ourselves, or some necessary law
of our thought by which our mental action is
irresistibly controlled. In geometry, for instance, we start from certain axioms regarding
space ; in arithmetic from certain notions con

cerning quantity; in logic from certain mental
conceptions; and the certainty of our conclusions
depends on these axioms, notions, and conceptions being what are called necessary truths;
that is, propositions to which we cannot help
assenting, and the contrary to which we find it
impossible to think. Nothing that lies outside
our own minds can possibly serve our purpose as
the starting-point of the reasoning which is to
land us in demonstrated truth ; because we know
nothing outside our minds except by inferences
from impressions made on our consciousness,
and the trustworthiness of such inferences is
matter only of practical assumption, and is incapable of any logical proof. We might reason
from an observed external fact with the utmost
accuracy, each link of the argument being irre-
futable; yet our conclusion would only be of the
same quality as our knowledge of the primary
fact; it would rest on observation as its ultimate
basis, and not be a demonstrated truth.

In seeking, then, to reason out the existence
of God, and place it on the firm basis of logical
proof, we must start from some necessary conception of our own minds, or law of our own
thought. But an insuperable difficulty at once
confronts us. If the primary axiom or truth
from which we start be internal to our own

minds, so also will be the conclusion at which we arrive. By drawing out all that our premiss contains, we shall ascertain what the laws of our own thought compel us to think, but nothing else whatever; to get out of ourselves by this process, and discover external, independent facts, is simply impossible. Beginning within ourselves, we should continue within ourselves, and end within ourselves, imprisoned always within the narrow circle of our own conceptions, and unable to get beyond the limits of our own individuality to assure ourselves of anything that actually exists in the wide universe without. Supposing then that our minds were to reason up to God as the outcome and result of their mode of thinking, we should be no nearer to possessing a demonstration of His actual Being.

Should it be urged that the laws of our mental processes are the measures of real existence, and that whatever our thought developes out of itself must have corresponding to it an independent external reality, the answer is obvious. It is certainly possible that the figments of our thought may be really true, and that the realities of the universe may correspond with the subjective conceptions which result from the operations of our own minds; but we cannot formulate any proof that it is so. To take it for granted would be to make an enormous assumption, for the validity of which not the most shadowy sort of case could be made out by the utmost efforts of the reasoning faculty. If the assumption can be justified, it must be on grounds which lie altogether outside the province of rigorous and absolute demonstration.

It is really a truth which only requires to be stated to obtain instant acceptance, that facts external to ourselves must be ascertained by observation, and cannot be discovered by processes of abstract reasoning from principles furnished by our own minds. Moreover, against the possibility of logically demonstrating from our own conceptions the fact of God's existence lies this additional difficulty, that our idea of God does not admit of that precise and formal definition which is necessary for the construction of a demonstrative argument. We cannot put eternity, infinity, and self-existence into our propositions as if they were manageable ideas, bounded on all sides and capable of being firmly grasped by our minds. They are too vast and indeterminate; we can only approximate to them by negations, and reach out towards them vaguely and tentatively, but reason rigorously concerning them we cannot.

When, therefore, it is objected by the agnostic

that the offered demonstrations of the existence
of God which are called *a priori*, as resting on
some law of our own thought, and not on observation of the external universe, fall short of their
mark and fail, the objection may be admitted
without prejudice to the cause of Theism. All
we need say is that such methods of proof are
by their very nature inapplicable to the case.
God cannot be the last term of a train of reasoning constructed out of our own mental conceptions. If He exists at all, He is a living Person,
not a logical conclusion. That such methods of
seeking Him fail creates no presumption that He
cannot be found.

Three of the kinds of proof mentioned and
pronounced insufficient by our agnostic have
now been briefly examined, and their inapplicability to the matter in hand shown to be inherent
in their nature; and we now come to the last,
the method of logical induction from the phenomena of the universe. This too is pronounced
inadequate; by this, as surely as by the rest, we
are told we shall fail to reach God.

Well, to that assertion we have already signi-
fied assent; and we go on to show that it cannot
be otherwise than true, simply for the reason
that this method also is in its nature inapplicable.

Let it, however, be clearly understood what precisely the assertion is to which we have assented. It is that God cannot be reached by logical induction from the phenomena of the universe. We do not say that those phenomena may not help us in our search for Him, may not testify intelligibly to reason concerning Him; on the contrary, they will be afterwards a most important element in our argument on behalf of Theism. Our agreement with the agnostic is strictly limited to his assertion of the failure of the method of *logical induction*. We shall hereafter endeavour to show that the existence of God is a fair, reasonable, and trustworthy inference to be drawn by the rational faculty in man from the phenomena of the universe; all we now admit is that it is not a strictly logical inference; in other words, that the living God cannot be the last term of a reasoned induction from physical phenomena.

This distinction implies an essential difference between inferences which are strictly logical and inferences which, though illogical, are practically reasonable and trustworthy; and it will be well to explain and justify it before we go further.

Every one is familiar with the fact, that while there are some inferences which can be drawn with such certainty that no sane or coherent

D

mind can withhold assent from them, provided
that it is competent to understand the process
by which they are drawn; there are other inferences of an entirely different kind, not admitting of any such irresistible proof, but depending
on estimates of probability and teachings of experience, which inferences, notwithstanding their
logical weakness, are unhesitatingly accepted by
all rational persons as sufficient grounds of action.
Of the former kind are the deductions of pure
reason; of the other the practical judgments by
which conduct is governed.

From the necessary conceptions of space, for
instance, the inference is drawn with irresistible
cogency that the sum of the angles of every
plane rectilinear triangle is equal to two right
angles. The proof consists of a series of propositions to each of which the mind cannot help
assenting, and the result has the validity of
absolute demonstration. But the inference from
his past conduct that a person is honest and may
safely be trusted is drawn by a different process
altogether, a process not of pure reasoning but
of practical judgment guided by experience; and
on inferences of this sort we habitually rely, and
consider them valid enough to be the foundation
of our sentiments and conduct, even in the most
important affairs of life.

It is a distinction of this nature which we make between a strictly logical induction, and a practically trustworthy inference, of the existence of God from physical phenomena. And we now go on to point out, by an examination of the several lines of such an induction, as commonly drawn out, that they do in fact fall short and fail; and that, as it might be anticipated from the nature of the case, no merely logical process can compel the mind to ascend from phenomena discerned by the senses, to an unseen and unique spiritual Cause from which they originate.

The lines of induction by which it might be attempted to prove the existence of God from the physical universe may be characterized as those of Causation, Order, and Design. By following each as far as it can lead us, we shall see that it necessarily falls short of its aim.

Let us first try the line of induction which starts from the idea of Causation.

From consciousness, or experience, or both combined, we derive the idea that whatever exists must have owed its existence to something which preceded it and was its cause. There is not a form of matter or a living creature or an event, which we can conceive of as having been un-caused. The like conviction equally holds good of the causes which brought the present exis-

tences into being; they too can only be viewed
by us as having originated in causes which preceded them. And in this way the necessity of
causation seems to stretch back indefinitely.
However far back we go on the line of causation,
we can never in thought reach a state of things
of which we can imagine that it had no cause.
But then how is the universe to be accounted
for? It must either have been eternal, an infinite succession of causes and effects without any
beginning; or it must have been the effect of
some self-existent uncaused first cause, beyond
which we cannot go.

Such is the dilemma in which our idea of
causation, however we come by it, inevitably
places us. And the question is, whether of the
two alternatives we are entitled to say that the
former is logically inadmissible, and the latter
demonstrably true. For if the inference of God
from our idea of causation possesses the certainty
of a demonstrated conclusion, it can only be because of these two alternatives we are shut up to
the latter as the only one which can be conceived
possible. But is this really so? On one view
we should have to conceive the universe to be
some vast organism or machine of which the
cause, if it have one, is in itself, and which
everlastingly goes on producing new phenomena.

On the other we should have to conceive of some eternal, self-existent, uncaused cause, outside and prior to the universe, and giving birth to it at some definite moment of Time. Now it is evident that both of these conceptions lie altogether outside the idea of causation with which we started. It is just as difficult, and as unwarranted by experience, to imagine an uncaused first cause, as an uncaused or self-caused universe. Before both one and the other of these conceptions our logical faculty stands dumb and powerless. Whatever grounds there may be for preferring one hypothesis to the other, of which we shall see more hereafter, it is manifest that our logical idea of causation will not of itself enable us to make a choice between them, and therefore cannot but fail to lead us with the certainty of demonstration to God as the uncaused Cause of all things.

We pass on to examine the line of induction which infers God from the Order manifest in the universe.

Experience teaches us, within its own sphere, to infer the action of mind or intelligence from the appearance of order. Materials scattered or piled together at random, suggest nothing but blind force; combined in regular forms they suggest a disposing and ordering intelligence.

But with this important limitation ; that the combinations are of the same, or a similar, kind as those which we know by experience to have been arranged by intelligence. When we have learnt what sorts of nests animals build, we securely infer the action of their intelligence or instinct from all similiar combinations of similar materials. A confused heap of letters of the alphabet may have resulted from their having been pitched down anyhow, for aught we can tell ; but when we observe them standing arranged in legible sentences, we cannot doubt that the human mind has been at work in ordering them. From order, then, we securely infer mind, when both the ordering mind and the ordered materials are of the kinds which lie within the domain of our experience.

But for the purpose of our induction we must go much beyond this ; and the question is whether we can extend the inference with certainty beyond the domain of experience into regions which lie outside of our practical knowledge. Nature presents us with magnificent and countless displays of order in all her provinces, from the smallest crystal and meanest flower up to planetary systems and stellar suns. But the origin of her order, and the power which

presides over her arrangements, are entirely beyond the limits of our experience. Can we then
pronounce with the confidence of assured knowledge that mind, and mind alone, has produced
her order ? That there is an analogy, a resemblance in some points of view, between her
arrangements and those due to human intelligence is undeniable, but the question is how far
such an analogy can lead us towards a demonstrated conclusion. Can it be unhesitatingly
affirmed, that our experience of the production
of order is wide and complete enough to exclude
any conceivable cause of order except mind?
Suppose it were suggested that Nature is a vast
unconscious organism, which by the unknown
law of its working is evermore bringing forth
in countless profusion the phenomena of order;
is our experience of the conscious production of
order by our own intelligence sufficient of itself
to prove the suggestion to be absurd? Surely
no one will contend that it is sufficient in the
strict logical sense, for the whole case is one
which lies beyond our experience, and to which
we can only reach out in a vague manner by
imperfect and insecure analogies. And if so,
then the inference of a divine Mind from the
order observed in the universe, though it may
approve itself to our instinctive sense of reality,

cannot possess the validity of a secure logical induction.

For a like reason the analogous inference from Design must also fall short of conclusive and irresistible proof. We know by familiar experience that human intelligence constructs mechanisms to serve particular purposes; it conceives a design, and then selects, shapes, and fits together certain materials in such a manner that all the parts of the structure conspire together to the intended end. Whenever, therefore, we meet with a piece of mechanism of the kind, speaking generally, which men are accustomed to make, we securely infer that a human mind has been at work to produce it. Turning, then, from the works of man to Nature, we meet with innumerable organisms which resemble pieces of mechanism in being composed of parts conspiring to effect some definite purpose ; and the thought inevitably occurs to us that if the piece of mechanism rightly indicates mind, so also must the mechanical organism. But just as before, the inference when examined is found to rest on an imperfect analogy, which is far from being able to bear the strain of a strictly reasoned induction. In no case can our observation discover how Nature's mechanical organisms are produced. The secret of their growth is impenetrable. Had we ascertained the action of mind in causing any of them, we might have argued securely to all the rest; but there is not one which betrays to our observation the hidden energy which gave it birth. To assert, then, that they too must be due to mind, and cannot be due to any other cause, would be to make a great leap beyond the limits within which our experience is able to guide us. So far as we can undertake legitimately to pronounce from our acquaintance with the things around us, these exquisite animal and vegetable mechanisms may possibly have been thrown out by unconscious Nature, revolving in her mysterious course in accordance with laws which are altogether beyond the reach of our science. Hence, however strongly the inference of God from the appearance of design in Nature may approve itself to our practical reason, it cannot possess the force of a demonstrated conclusion.

We have now concisely passed under review the several kinds of proof suggested by the agnostic as conceivable, and pronounced by him to be inadequate; namely, direct observation by the senses, scientific physical investigation, reasoning from the ultimate laws or conceptions of our own minds, logical induction from the idea of causation, and from the evidences of order and design in Nature. The result so far has been to arrive at a certain measure of agreement with his position, that the existence of God is incapable of proof. If by proof be meant logical demonstration, the drawing of a conclusion from unquestionable premisses by a chain of unanswerable reasoning, every link of which compels assent, in that sense we must allow that God cannot be proved by us to exist.

But here we part company. Whereas the agnostic ends his inquiry here, and dismisses God from his thoughts as a Being of whom it is impossible for us to know even the bare existence; we start from this point on a new quest, and feel sure that God can be found with sufficient and practical certainty, though not in the way of logical demonstration. Why we hold that the failure to prove rigorously the existence of God by no means closes the inquiry, nor establishes the impossibility of finding in the knowledge of His goodness and love the repose for which our hearts cry out, must be reserved for explanation in the next chapter.

CHAPTER III.

THE INSUFFICIENCY OF LOGICAL METHODS TO ESTABLISH PRIMARY TRUTHS.

Our task in this chapter may be compared to that of a military strategist, who has to make good a retreat from a position which is found untenable, to another where he may renew the conflict, and hope to bring it to a successful termination. We have conceded the impracticability of proving the existence of God by rigorous logic and demonstrative induction; and we have now to show why we do not consider the controversy as ended by this concession, but only transferred to another ground, where we still look forward to conducting it to an affirmative issue.

Our general reason for refusing to regard the failure to find logical or demonstrative proof of God's existence decisive of the question whether He can be known by us, is the certain and manifest inapplicability of the whole method of logical proof to the matter which we have in hand. This has partly appeared already, but requires more attentive consideration.

If we reflect on the nature of logical processes, we shall presently see that they can never carry us out of the sphere in which their premisses lie. Within the domain in which they commence, they must also end. Beginning with one kind of subject-matter, they cannot land us in conclusions respecting another of a different kind. From axioms about space, for instance, they cannot deduce ethical truths; from properties of numbers they cannot lead us to the laws of beauty. As well might we put corn into a mill, and expect to grind out gunpowder, as reason from premisses which concern one subject or class of things, and hope to arrive at conclusions about some quite different subject or class.

Now the premisses from which we can start in our logical processes must be derived from one of two sources; either from our own minds, or from the phenomena which we perceive to be external to us. There is no other source available, for these two comprise everything which our logical understanding can know and handle. Within is the Self, of which we are conscious; outside is the Not-Self, the rest of the universe, known to us through our sensations, and known only in its phenomena.   One or other of these must supply the premisses of our demonstrative reasonings, according to the well-known maxim, "There is nothing in the intellect but was first in the senses, except the intellect itself."

Suppose we take our premisses from the former source, the Self of which we are conscious, and argue from some law of our own thought, or some conception or idea framed by our own minds.   Then the conclusion which we reach will, as we have already seen, be bounded by the limits of the Self.   It will, of necessity, be as subjective, to employ the technical term, as the premisses were; it will be a truth of our minds, a truth of reason as distinguished from experience; an ideal truth, altogether distinct and apart from the world of external reality. There is no logical process nor direct intellectual perception by which any such conclusion can be shown to have a corresponding reality in the Not-Self, the universe outside the human mind; and if from the subjective conception or result we make a bold leap to objective existence in the actual world, it is a leap which has no sanction from the principles of strict, demonstrative reasoning.

Or suppose we take our premisses from the other source, the external world known to us in

its phenomena by means of our sensations.
Here, then, we are in the region of physics, and
out of that region we cannot escape. If from
the phenomena we demonstrate causes, they will
be physical causes; if laws, they will be physical
laws. Whatever be our results, they must
belong to the same sphere as the premisses, that
is, to the physical sphere; to that we shall be
inextricably bound by the very nature of the
processes of strict inductive reasoning.

Hence to enable us to arrive at God, and
establish His existence by such a series of linked
propositions as form a demonstration, He would
need to be one of these two objects; either a
conclusion from the necessary laws or conceptions
of our own minds, or a Being belonging to the
sphere of physics, and revealed through physical
phenomena apprehended by our senses. But
such a God would have nothing in common with
the glorious Being whose idea fills our souls
with adoring emotion, and of whose real existence we are seeking evidence. What we are
thinking of is a purely spiritual Personality;
an infinite Mind whom Time and Space cannot
circumscribe; a primal Cause, not in the physical sense, but by the power of an omnipotent
volition, acting on the universe by a force which
is not physical, but wholly supernatural and

spiritual. Had the God of our belief been conceived of as a mere logical necessity of thought,
we might have hoped to demonstrate His existence from the structure of our own minds; had
He been present to our minds as the first of a
chain of physical causes or laws, we might have
hoped to arrive at Him by an induction from
the phenomena of the universe; and when we
had sought Him by these methods in vain, and
He was nowhere to be found, the failure would
have been a very serious reason for doubting of
His existence. But a failure to find the living
God, by methods which we know beforehand to
be inapplicable and doomed to inevitable barren-
ness, counts for nothing. It cannot justly
originate even the slightest presumption against
His existence, any more than it can in favour
of it. It has no bearing on the great question
at all. It leaves us entirely free to start again
on the search for Him by more promising and
suitable methods, and to hope that by these we
may be able to find Him.

But the grave inquiry then faces us, whether
there are other methods open to us; whether,
when we have abandoned the purely logical
ground, there is any other on which a stand for
belief in God can be made. The discouraging
question starts up to bar our way: " Is not our

real knowledge necessarily limited to things of the existence of which we can obtain such proof as our logical understanding can rest in, convinced and satisfied ; and must not all else that we think or talk about be mere guess or fancy, too unstable to be a ground of action, too flimsy and dream-like to be worthy of serious consideration ? "

Such is the question which the agnostic confidently asks, and triumphantly answers in the affirmative. " You form an idea of God," he says to us, " but of any corresponding objective reality you confess yourselves unable to formulate a proof. Why not resign yourselves to the inevitable inference, that the God of your conception is nothing but the offspring of your idealizing faculty, without substance or independent existence ; and that if there should chance to be any real God behind the universe, at least He lies altogether beyond the reach of your faculties, and outside the possibilities of human knowledge ? "

No doubt there is an air of plausibility about the view which thus rudely smites back the yearning of our hearts for God, and condemns us to perpetual imprisonment within the bounds of our physical existence. If it were just, the controversy would be ended, and to try other methods of finding God, after the failure of the logical and demonstrative methods, would be waste of time and labour. To justify, therefore, our perseverance in the search, we must show that this view of the necessary limits of human knowledge is unsound, and contradicts both experience and reason.

We affirm it to be so on this distinct ground, that the principle which it embodies would, if accepted, make a clean and absolute sweep of all human knowledge whatsoever. This statement we proceed to justify.

The principle against which we protest may be expressed as follows :—Knowledge must be based on logical proof; the knowable and the demonstrable are identical ; whatever cannot be shown by strict inductive reasoning to exist must be dismissed from the region of science, and consigned to the dream-land of the speculative imagination. Our contention is that as soon as this principle, which is really the stronghold of agnosticism, is tried at the bar of the practical reason, and brought face to face with the realities of human life, it must be convicted of monstrous absurdity.

Nothing is more certain than that every train of reasoning must have some premiss from which to start. Arguments cannot sustain

E

themselves in the air, without any basis to rest
upon, real or assumed. Logical processes without materials to work upon can no more bring
forth results in the shape of knowledge, than a
mill can grind out flour without being supplied
with grist. But whence shall we fetch the
indispensable premisses to set our arguments
agoing? If it be said that they are furnished
by previous trains of argument by means of
which they have been established, we must
again ask whence the premisses for these were
obtained; nor can we cease reiterating the question, until in each case we reach some premiss
which was antecedent to every logical process,
and was the original material on which the
reasoning faculty began to operate. And how
did we get these? Not by reasoning, for the
argument could not begin until the mind was in
possession of them. Whatever they were, or
from whatever source they were obtained, they
were certainly not the product of any logical
process or reasoned induction. They were the
primitive elements of thought, the starting-
points of knowledge, the foundation of all the
science of which man is capable. And they
were not the result of any sort of reasoning. If
they were trustworthy and true, then we possess
real knowledge which was not derived from

reasoning, and is not capable of logical demonstration. If they were not trustworthy and
true, then none of our pretended knowledge is
trustworthy and true, for upon them every
particle of it ultimately depends; in a word, it
is not knowledge at all. So that we are driven
perforce to choose between these alternatives;
either we know nothing at all, or we know more
than we can prove.

Now it is by no means impossible for the
metaphysical recluse to argue himself down into
utter and absolute scepticism about everything
in heaven and earth. So long as he shuts himself up from human society and employment,
and forgets in what sort of world he is living,
he may go on weaving the web of fanciful
speculation, and drifting unconsciously from one
absurdity to another, till existence itself assumes
to his distempered mind the aspect of an uneasy
dream. But a touch of reality disperses the
mist, and reduces these vagaries of thought to
their proper level. The record which the great
sceptic of the last century, David Hume, has
left us of his own experience in this respect is as
instructive as it is amusing. Let us listen to
what he writes about himself.

" The *intense* view of these manifold contradictions and imperfections in human reason has

E 2

so wrought upon me and heated my brain, that
I am ready to reject all belief and reasoning,
and can look upon no opinion as more probable
or likely than another. Where am I, or what?
From what causes do I derive my existence,
and to what condition shall I return? Whose
favour shall I covet, and whose anger must
I dread? What beings surround me? and
on whom have I any influence, or who has
any influence on me? I am confounded with
all these questions, and begin to fancy myself
in the most deplorable condition imaginable,
environed with the deepest darkness, and utterly
deprived of the use of every member and
faculty."

" Most fortunately it happens," he goes on to
say, " that since reason is incapable of dispelling
these clouds, Nature herself suffices to that purpose, and cures me of this philosophical melancholy and delirium, either by relaxing this bent
of mind, or by some avocation and lively impression of my senses, which obliterate all these
chimeras. I drive, I play a game of back-
gammon, I converse and am merry with my
friends; and when, after three or four hours'
amusement I would return to these speculations,
they appear so cold and strained and ridiculous,
that I cannot find in my heart to enter into

them any farther." (*Treatise on Human Nature,*
book i., part iv. sect. 7.)

A curious spectacle, in this busy world of
action and affection, of toil and hope, is the
thorough-going metaphysical dreamer, launch-
ing himself down the steep incline of scepticism,
with the resolve to cast away every shred of
belief for which he cannot find some secure
logical basis or proof. One hardly knows
whether to laugh or cry over him, when at last
he lies shivering in utter nakedness at the
bottom.

First of all goes, of course, his belief in the
entire material or physical universe. What to
him are the constellations of mighty orbs which
pour their quenchless radiance through the immensities of space? What the ordered system
of worlds which circle majestically round our
central sun, and the familiar home of the
human family, this solid earth with its steadfast
mountains, luxuriant plains, and vast billowy
expanses of ocean? The tribes of animated
Nature thronging earth and air and water, the
stately forests, the blooming garniture of spring,
the profusion of ripening fruits, the endless di-
versities of form and colour and texture, to him
what too are these? Substantial realities,
which he can gaze upon with rapture, and use

with satisfaction and thankfulness? Vain
fancy! To him they are but sensations of his
own brain, transient thrills of his own nerves,
momentary states of his individual consciousness.
To him sight and hearing and touch are nothing
but vibrations of something belonging to himself,
caused he knows not how, and meaning he knows
not what. For between these sensations of
which he is conscious, and any imagined external world, no logic can bridge over the chasm,
no reasoned induction establish a communica-
tion. The physical universe must therefore be
surrendered as an unsubstantial dream. Space
is emptied of its contents, nay itself is reduced
but to a figment of his own consciousness.

In this strange desolation, however, this
waste and drear desert of Vacuity, may he not
at least enjoy the solace of other minds to bear
him company and cheer him with a reciprocated
sympathy? Other minds, do we say? Why
to him there can be no other! Does genius
flash from the page? The page itself is but a
sensation of his own. Do the accents of truth
and wisdom fall on his ears? It is but a thrill
of his own nerves of which he is sensible. Does
a loving face beam on him with tenderness, a
loving voice whisper to him of affection and
constancy? The face, the voice, are nothing to

him but flickering movements of his own consciousness. A mind to answer to his own is a
phantom which eludes his grasp. Nohow can
his boasted logic lay hold of it. It too must
go ; and in the midst of an annihilated universe,
if the expression may be allowed, must his mind
sit solitary, self-centred and supreme in its
loneliness.

But stay! His mind,—can he keep even
that ? Can he prove to himself that he is himself at all, or possesses any Self to argue about ?
True to his principle he is bound to do summary
execution on himself, and commit intellectual
suicide. Before his remorseless logic his own
existence is reduced to the conception of a succession of momentary states of consciousness.
between which no bond of connexion can be
perceived. A permanent Self to which they
belong, linking them together as successive portions of individual experience, would be an assumption illogical enough to draw a shriek of
indignant protest from whatever faculty can be
supposed to remain in his possession. He is not
entitled even to say at any instant, " I existed a
moment ago;" for all that he is conscious of is
the Present, and memory itself is but a sensation
of the passing moment, to which it cannot be
proved that any real Past corresponds. He

must therefore resign the Past as incapable of proof; and since the unrealized future can be nothing but a dream of fancy or hope, all he has left him to exist in is the moment of his actually present consciousness. Let us imagine, if we can, a succession of instantaneous, unconnected flashes out of the gloom of nothingness; it is to some such incoherent and unsubstantial phantom that our metaphysician will be pared down by his fatal logic, which may be said to plunder him of his human birthright, strip off his personality, and leave him more than half annihilated.

How hollow and unpractical all such subtleties of speculative thought appear, when we return into the atmosphere and bustle of real life ! Here we know ourselves to be living men, tenants of a magnificent world the structure and laws of which our intellect explores, and the various substances and products of which we gather and subdue to our use. Here we feel ourselves to be linked to our fellow-men by a thousand ties, mind answering to mind and heart to heart, the individual being a member of a family, the family of a nation, the nation of the entire race. Here each of us is conscious of his own incommunicable personality, endowed with reason, will, and conscience, a mysterious and sacred microcosm; and in the power of this permanent personality we walk amidst Nature as its lords, interpreting it by the prerogative of mind, discerning its purpose, inferring its Past, divining its Future. This is reality, this is human life, as we know them by an experience which cannot be fallacious.

All this life, this reality, rest on knowledge which is prior to logical processes, and is obtained through our consciousness. We do not reason it out; it comes to us, and we possess it and live by it. We trust our intuitions, our perceptions, our experience; that is the secret of our practical, our human life. In the sphere of this life the question, " Can you prove demonstratively the grounds on which you act ? " turns out to be an idle one. Were we to wait till we could answer it in the affirmative, death would overtake us before we had begun to live.

The bearing of the foregoing discussion on the momentous problem before us, the possibility of our ever arriving at a sufficient and practical knowledge of God, is too close to need many words in explanation of it. We confessed that we could not demonstrate God logically; and the rejoinder was, " Then give up the expectation of knowing Him at all." Nay, we reply, we are something higher and better than logical machines, which can do nothing but grind out demonstrations, or else rust in the ignorance of scepticism. We are human beings who have other inlets of knowledge than the logical understanding, and who certainly know more than we can rigorously prove. Our entire lives rest on principles and facts which come to us through no process of reasoning, but by intuition and perception, and the lessons of experience; on these we act without troubling ourselves about demonstrations and reasoned proofs, and it is only by accepting them as trustworthy and true that we live human lives, and escape herding with the beasts or the insane. Through the same inlets of knowledge, then, it may be that God will be revealed to us; and till we have sought Him through these we should be less than human if we abandoned the search for Him, and resigned ourselves to drag on a dreary existence in the inhospitable deserts of atheism.

Whenever therefore, in our search for evidences of God, we are assailed by objections which not only strike at the grounds of theism, but, if admitted, would be equally fatal to all the beliefs by which our lives as human beings are regulated, we shall feel ourselves entitled to put such objections aside as irrelevant and undeserving of serious attention. ` We cannot soberly treat

it as an open question, whether the physical
universe really exists, or whether there are any
other minds than our own, or whether we ourselves are anything more than melting mists of
successive perceptions without any permanent
Self to be the subject of them. If we did not
take these things for granted on the veracity of
our consciousness, discussions about theism and
everything else would be nothing but vanity
and vexation of spirit.

For a similar reason we shall hold ourselves
excused from making any account of objections
to the idea of God which are founded on the
alleged impossibility of conceiving, or explaining
the existence of, an infinite, eternal Personality.
Is space finite or infinite? If finite, who can
conceive what lies beyond it? If infinite, who
can comprehend it at all? Yet we cannot help
assuming its existence, we cannot dispense with
belief in it. Again, is the universe eternal, or
had it a beginning in time? If the former, who
can form an idea of its Past? If the latter, who
can imagine what was before it? Yet it must
be believed by us to exist, and our lives are based
on the assumption of its reality. So we may
summon up a number of so-called inconceivables
and inexplicables, which in spite of the in-
ability of our finite minds to frame rounded and

complete ideas of them, or to explain their modes and grounds of existence, not only constrain us to believe in them, but actively mould and shape our lives. In the name then of consistency and reason, why should we stumble at the idea of God on the ground that our thought is unequal to comprehend or explain an infinite and eternal Personality?

CHAPTER IV.

THE METHOD OF CONSCIOUSNESS, AND ITS APPLICATION TO THE SEARCH FOR GOD.

WE approach now the constructive part of our inquiry into the grounds of our belief in God. Having dismissed the strictly logical or demonstrative method as inadequate and inapplicable, we turn now to the very different method of ascertaining facts and forming beliefs, which furnishes us with the primary knowledge lying underneath the whole fabric of our human life. This may be called the method of consciousness; and in the present chapter we propose to give some account of its nature, and of the way in which it may be applied to the establishment of theism.

We have seen that prior to and beneath all our logical processes there are beliefs and convictions which spring up in the human consciousness, and are the only possible foundation of all our knowledge. They are felt to be true, though formally to prove them true is impossible. We take them on the veracity of our consciousness, and build our life upon them without hesitation or distrust. They may be called instinctive or intuitive, to indicate their being rooted in our mental constitution, and to distinguish them from beliefs which are attained through logical processes. Or they may be fitly called primary beliefs of the reason, as being convictions which approve themselves to the rational faculty of men in general by their own fitness, and are the basis on which it erects the superstructure of acquired knowledge.

Now these primary or instinctive beliefs must be held to be indisputable, because they form the only barrier between our minds and the bottomless gulf of absolute and universal scepticism. If then theism can establish its right to be considered one of their number, it will be proved in the only practicable sense, and will rest on the same foundation as the most certain parts of our knowledge.

The proof, therefore, which we shall endeavour to draw out on behalf of theism will consist of various arguments, all directed to show that belief in God is entitled to be considered one of the primary, instinctive or intuitive beliefs of the human reason.

But these primary beliefs, — what is their character, and how may they be ascertained and distinguished from other beliefs? If to be rightly numbered among them constitutes a valid claim for a belief to be accepted as true, it must be of the first importance to have some definition of their character by which to test the claimant for admission into their number. Their general characteristics must therefore be a preliminary object of our examination.

A little reflection will show, we think, that these primary beliefs are of more kinds than one. Those which have their origin directly in the senses are the simplest, the most inevitable, the most universal. They take possession of all men in whom reason exists. There is probably not a savage of the meanest degree of intellect who has the smallest doubt of the reality of the external world, or who would not laugh to scorn the idea of such a doubt if it could by any means be brought within his comprehension. Even of beliefs which do not originate in the senses, but spring up directly out of the consciousness, at least one, that of personal identity, is as universal as human reason. There is probably not a sane person in the world who does not believe that all through the vicissitudes of his experience he remains the same person, and continues to be

himself. But the case of moral and spiritual
beliefs is somewhat different. These are more
complex, and more dependent on the state or
culture of the individual. We can conceive of
savages so debased and so little human as to have
no capacity for entertaining such beliefs at all.
We can conceive of persons not destitute of
knowledge and cultivation, in whom either the
moral or the religious faculty has been so starved
and stunted by unfavourable circumstances that
their hearts make no response to sentiments
which command the general assent of mankind.
So again there are beliefs which belong to a
tolerably advanced state of human culture, and
are not reached in its earlier stages, but which,
when they are at last worked out, assert such an
irresistible affinity for the mind, and root themselves in it so firmly and ineradicably, as to prove
themselves to be truly instinctive beliefs of the
reason. Such, for instance, is the modern conviction of the universal reign of Law in Nature,
by which, in our own days, the idea of chance
has been utterly banished from the whole sphere
of scientific thought.

When, therefore, we inquire for the primary
and instinctive beliefs of the reason, which underlie all logical proof, and must be accepted on
the veracity of the consciousness, we have no

right absolutely to limit the class to beliefs which have been actually held by all men, at all times and in every quarter. The test of such complete universality would be too exclusive. Some persons are defective in one or more of the senses, but the exception does not deprive the senses of their right to be deemed essential parts of human nature. Some barbarous tribes seem to lack all true perception of beauty, and yield their admiration to forms which are hideous and disgusting; there are nevertheless laws of art and conditions of beauty rooted in the mental constitution, which only need cultivation for their development. So when humanity exists in a rudimentary state, as among ignorant, uncivilized tribes, or in a maimed and mutilated condition, as in individuals who are deficient in one or other of the superior human affections or principles of conduct; the absence in such tribes or individuals of a belief which is common to the great mass of educated and well-grown minds is by no means conclusive against the title of that belief to be considered an instinctive or indigenous belief, proper to and inseparable from the ideal of humanity.

In fact, we need not perplex ourselves here with many questions which might be raised about a belief; whether it is innate, or acquired

F

by experience, or stimulated by observation, or transmitted by heredity, or actually held by all men of every class and character, or is the result of one kind of culture rather than of another. The one essential point is the relation of the belief to the general human conscious-ness. Does it grow up there as a natural, spon-taneous product, asserting itself in the healthy mind as an original, native perception of truth, independent of logical proof; and does it go on rooting itself more deeply with every accession of experience, so as to evince its organic affinity with the constitution of human nature? If so, then it is entitled to be reckoned one of those primary beliefs of the reason which underlie all reasoning, and justify themselves by their existence.

This expression, "justify themselves by their existence," may at first appear strange and pro-voke incredulity; but it really expresses a fact from which there is no escape except by aban-doning beliefs of every kind. Our primary, practical, working beliefs, which spring up of themselves directly out of our consciousness matured by experience, must justify themselves, for no other justification of them is possible. Why do we believe in our own personality, in the minds of our fellow-men, and in a physical universe, but because we believe in them and cannot help believing in them? It is idle to protest that the inference from the subjective impression to the objective reality is illogical and untrustworthy; in these primary intuitions all the world makes it, and cannot help making it; and " *Securus judicat orbis terrarum,*" it is vain to protest against a unanimous world.

Our position therefore is this: that if the belief in God can be shown to be a primary, instinctive, and practically universal belief of the reason, like those beliefs which have just now been mentioned,—a belief growing up of itself, so to speak, in the consciousness, and continually deriving nourishment from experience and reflection,—it will need no further justification. Being such, it would justify itself.

Throughout the inquiry which we are about to make into the title of theistic belief to be ranked among the great primary beliefs of the reason, the importance of the fact will be manifest to which attention was directed at the outset; the fact that the idea of God is supreme in the whole field of thought, and touches human nature at every point with a unique and sovereign authority. For it follows that if the idea is a true one, and the Being who is portrayed in it really exists and stands to mankind in this supreme and universal relation, every part of human nature and life will be affected by His existence, and may be expected to exhibit traces of His presence and action, and thus to bear witness that He really is.

Let us try to make this thought clearer, by using an illustration borrowed from physical science.

There is one idea in physics which embraces the whole material universe, without excepting a single particle of its substance. We mean, of course, the idea of gravitation, the idea that every atom of matter attracts (or behaves itself as if it attracted, which is practically the same thing) all other atoms with a force proportioned to its own mass, and varying inversely as the square of the distance. This, according to the idea, is a universal property of matter, whether it blazes in stars and suns, revolves in planetary orbs, floats in the atmosphere, swims in the oceans, constitutes the organisms of animal or vegetable life, is solid or fluid or gaseous. If then the idea be true, there is not a mass of matter, large or small, which, when questioned by the instruments of physical research, ought not to yield evidence of its truth. The motions of the binary stars round each other in the immensities of space ought to accord with it; the courses of the planets round the sun, and of the satellites round their primaries, and the perturbations which arise from their mutual interactions, ought to bear witness to it. In the fall of bodies to the earth, and the difference of their weights at the equator and the poles; in the change of rate of the pendulum when carried down to the bottom of a mine; in the decrease of density, and the lowering of the boiling-point, in the upper regions of the atmosphere, and the increase of pressure in the ocean depths; in the rise of the mercury in the barometer and of the water in the pump; in these and hundreds of other phenomena testimony ought to be found to the objective truth of the idea. And we know how science has laboriously verified it. In the heights and the depths, wherever material bodies can be observed and their behaviour examined and registered, the ardent explorers of Nature's secrets have sought confirmations of the ideal law; and having found them everywhere, have accepted the law of gravitation as one of the most certain facts of the material universe.

Now let us conceive a similar method of verification applied to the great idea of God. We possess the idea, as we had that of gravitation; and in consequence of its character of supremacy and universality it is as applicable to every part of man's consciousness and experience, as the idea of gravitation is to every part of the substance of the material universe. Just then, as the influence and effect of gravitation are traceable everywhere in nature; so, if God be a fact, the impress and consequences of His Being ought to be traceable in man, and each province of human thought and knowledge, emotion and action, should yield evidence of His sovereign presence and operation.

Hence in our search for tokens of God and evidences of His Being, we are not limited to any one domain of experience, or any single province of human consciousness. Whatever man knows, whatever he perceives and feels, whatever experience the individual or the race has passed through—all is pertinent to the subject; in all, if God really is, we may hope to find some sign, more or less appreciable, of His existence.

Before we dismiss the physical illustration, we may derive from it a caution against making complete comprehension by the intellectual faculty the test of truth and reality. The law of gravitation is an irresistible inference from the observed phenomena of the material universe; that matter behaves itself universally in accordance with that law, is a conclusion which no

competent investigator can refuse to accept.
Yet the mode in which the law is sustained, the
force which acts and the means by which it acts,
are enveloped in impenetrable mystery. That
matter should act on distant matter, without any
intervening material medium to convey the
impulse or force, is simply unthinkable. Yet
there is not a particle which does not somehow
act on every other particle, even across distances
at which thought is staggered, and with a swift-
ness of effect compared with which, according to
the most recent researches, even the speed of light
itself is sluggish. What a gulf then may possibly separate practical acquaintance with facts
from a comprehension of their ultimate nature, or
of the grounds on which they rest! The secret
of the infinite Personality of God may be incomprehensible by our intellect, and the mode in
which He acts on the universe may be utterly
inexplicable and inconceivable; yet all the while
the heavens may truly declare to us His glory,
the earth with all its tribes repeat the strain,
and from the depths of our consciousness may be
echoed back the confession that He is indeed
the Living and the True, "the blessed and
only Potentate, the King of kings and Lord of
lords."

Our task now, in order to establish the pri-

mary, self-justifying character of theistic belief,
is to trace a more or less distinct witness to God
in the several provinces of human consciousness,
as developed and matured by experience and
reflection. As a preliminary to this search, it
will be helpful if we can form some antecedent
notion of the kinds of evidence we might expect
to discover, supposing the existence of God to
be a supreme fact. This accordingly shall be
our endeavour in the remainder of this chapter.

The question immediately before us may be
stated in this way. Given man on one side, and
God on the other, of what character would the
result in the human consciousness probably be?
How would the fact of God's existence be likely
to make itself felt by man? By what inlets
might we expect that infinite spiritual reality
to enter into human thought and experience?

In trying tentatively to arrive at a proximate
answer, we must first set before our minds the
nature of man as revealed in his consciousness;
then the accepted idea of God; and lastly, conceiving these in relation to each other, we must
endeavour, by means of analogy and experience,
to form a conjecture of the ways in which the
presence and operation of such a Being, if real
and not merely ideal, might be borne in on
man's mind and heart.

We begin with sketching out the nature of man as revealed in his consciousness, just noting the leading features of his personality as made known to him through self-introspection and experience.

We look into ourselves, and are in the first place conscious of an efficient Will. We originate volitions, and execute them; we are sensible of effort as a cause, and we observe effects following our efforts, trains of consequences originated and set in motion by them. Thus we learn that our will is a true cause, and that productive energy is an attribute of our personality.

Next, we are conscious of Intelligence. We discern the difference between order and disorder, between chaos and cosmos, between haphazard juxta-position and methodical arrangement. We contrive and adapt; we design mechanical structures of which the several parts conspire to an end; we conceive purposes, and carry them out by appropriate means; we perceive fitnesses in the collocation of parts, and beauty in harmonies of form and colour; we draw inferences, we comprehend and interpret. Thus we realize that to our personality belongs Mind, the faculty which foresees, purposes, and understands.

Further, we are conscious of a Moral element in our nature. Right and Wrong are not unmeaning words to us, but express intense, commanding realities. The law of Duty asserts its sovereign rights in our hearts, even when we disobey and defy it. We are not ignorant of the satisfactions of conscious rectitude, nor of the shame of self-reproach and guilt. We cannot rid ourselves of the sense of responsibility, without degrading ourselves below the level of humanity. In the midst of our passions sits Conscience in mysterious supremacy, with the terrible scourge of Remorse to avenge its slighted authority. We cannot refuse our approbation to truth and goodness, nor withhold our condemnation from meanness, falsehood, and injustice. Thus we know ourselves to be moral, responsible beings, with a moral law of supreme authority and sacredness impressed upon and energizing within our personality.

Lastly, we are conscious of an element in our nature which transcends even the moral element, and may be distinguished as Spiritual. It is this which soars highest, and reaches out farthest. It refuses to be satisfied with what is finite and transient, and strives to apprehend the infinite and the eternal. It is this which humanizes our affections, lifting them out of the sphere of instinct into the region of spirit.

By this our emotions of hope and desire and love are purged from the grossness of the flesh, and transmuted into spiritual forces, the springs of purest and holiest action. It is this which is the seat of Religion. It frames the idea of God, and prompts us humbly to adore Him, and to seek in Him the completion and repose of our being. Mysterious and undefinable, it pervades our nature, elevating our instincts, supplementing our intelligence, and touching our morality with the light and warmth of religion. It is that part of our being which most begets in us a vague sense of some divine kindred and everlasting destiny; and by our consciousness of it we complete the idea of our personality, and conceive ourselves to be spiritual beings.

Such is man, as discovered to himself by reflection on the several chief parts of his consciousness. That is, man when developed by culture, taught by experience, and trained in self-knowledge. For to know what human nature really is, we must take it at its best, and examine it when matured under favourable conditions. To go back to the primitive, untutored savage for the knowledge of man's constitution and powers would be as absurd as to go back to the acorn to become acquainted with the giant oak. Man, unfolded

and matured by cultivation, finds himself
to be a person, endowed with these four
cardinal elements of being; an efficient Will,
originating and acting; an intelligent Mind,
comprehending, designing, and interpreting; a
Moral Judgment, discerning between right and
wrong, enforced by the sacred authority of conscience, and accompanied by a sense of responsibility; and a Spiritual Faculty, which
strives to apprehend the infinite, exalts the
emotions and affections above the region of the
flesh and its instincts, and reaches out after an
ideal perfection and satisfaction in God. Such
is man, knit together in fellowship with his
fellow-men, and environed by the splendours
and harmonies, the adaptations and utilities, of
the physical universe.

Over against this portraiture of man we are
now to set the accepted idea of God. By this
sacred name we mean, of course, not the object of
worship before which the savage or the idolater
bows down, but the Divine Being whose glory
and perfection fill the enlightened and cultivated
mind; not the God of superstition, nor even of
systematic theology, but of the purest and most
spiritual Christian consciousness.

Of this idea of God the first feature
is Omnipotent Will, energizing in produc-

tion and government and accomplishment of purpose, throughout all the realms of the universe. '

The next is Infinite Intelligence, the principle of all order, the skill of all design, the perception of all existence and all possibility, the perfection of foresight, knowledge, and wisdom.

Thirdly comes Moral Perfection; infinite righteousness, purity, and truth; unchangeable steadfastness of character, in which is "no variableness neither shadow of turning;" absolute light, wherein is no darkness at all.

Lastly, as the summit and crown of divine excellence, comes the attribute of Fatherliness; inexhaustible richness of goodness, tenderness, and love.

These four features or attributes, Will, Mind, Moral perfectness, loving Fatherhood, in their highest conceivable development, centred in an infinite, eternal, spiritual Personality, make up the Christian idea of God.

We are about to imagine this idea actually realized in a supreme Being, and to consider in what ways the fact of His existence would, in that case, be likely to be borne in on the human consciousness. But it will be proper to notice here a preliminary objection, which is urged by the agnostic against our supposing that such a conception of God can have any objective reality.

"What you call your idea of God," he says, "is obviously nothing else than a magnified and non-natural man. You idealize human nature, taking its better elements for your materials, and omitting the worse; and having constructed as perfect a man as you are able to conceive, you enlarge the imaginary figure indefinitely, and name it God. Is not this too unreal and fantastic a process to give you the faintest clue to what God really may be?"

This is the old objection of anthropomorphism, which if substantiated would strip the idea of God of every attribute, and reduce it to a single incomprehensible word, the "Absolute." For it is manifestly impossible for us even to conceive of any attribute as existing in God, still less to recognize the exercise of it, unless we are conscious of possessing in ourselves a like attribute, an attribute of the same nature and kind, however imperfect may be the degree of its development within us.

That this limitation is unquestionable a moment's reflection will discover.

Acquainted with the action of our own senses, we can conceive of other creatures being endowed with similar organs of sense of much greater capacity and acuteness than ours; but to picture them to our thought as possessing and using some additional and entirely different sense we find impossible. Again, we can imagine beings having faculties, affections, powers of the same nature as those which we are conscious of possessing, only in other proportions and other degrees; but beings of a totally different constitution from our own are simply unimaginable by us. And why? Because the faculty in us which creates ideal forms, transcending our actual experience, must still borrow its materials from experience. The materials supplied by experience it may freely sort and arrange in every kind of combination and proportion, constructing out of them superhuman and ideal forms; but to invent an entirely new material of which experience had given no hint would be as impossible as to conceive of the inconceivable. We should have neither means of comprehending it, nor language to describe it.

Anthropomorphism, therefore, in the sense of rising to a conception of God from an idealization of man, is inevitable, if we are to conceive of God's character at all. We have no materials to portray Him with, besides those which are furnished by our own nature. If a revelation were made of some attributes in Him to which we had nothing corresponding in ourselves, it would be utterly unintelligible; it would reveal nothing. Hence the truth, that it is only from the knowledge of ourselves that we can rise to the knowledge of God.

Why, however, the impossibility of our conceiving of God at all, except as arrayed with attributes which exist very imperfectly in ourselves, should be a valid objection to our believing that He really exists, it is extremely hard to perceive. To help us to see how the case stands, let us again have recourse to an illustration.

By observing and generalizing from numerous specimens of mankind, I can produce in my mind an ideal of the human form more perfect and beautiful than any individual who has fallen under my notice. This ideal is my subjective conception, existing in my thought without possessing any external reality. But what right should I have to argue, that because my idealizing faculty has given birth to this conception, no reality answering to it can possibly exist, or at least be ascertained to exist? Let an exquisitely sculptured Greek statue be placed before me; dare I assert that it cannot be a real object because it realizes my ideal. Or better still, let a living Antinöus walk into my presence; shall I deny him to be a man, and contend that he can be nothing more than the visible phantom of my own thought, because his form corresponds to my conception of perfect human beauty ?

By parity, then, of reasoning, when from our observation of human nature we have in thought gathered together its noblest lineaments, divested them of every limitation, raised them to the highest elevation we can imagine, and centred them in an infinite Personality, thus forming to ourselves that absolute ideal of spiritual perfection which we call God; what right should we have to say to those who declare that they have found a real God of like perfection, " Impossible ! that is our ideal, and therefore it cannot be real." Surely, as far as any inference at all could be drawn from the action of our idealizing faculty, it would lie in the opposite direction. If human nature is such that by abstracting and generalizing from it we are able to frame an ideal God; if it actually possesses such personality, will, mind, moral and spiritual affections, as to provide the materials out of which our idealizing faculty can construct a conception of absolute perfection; this richly-endowed nature of ours has to be accounted for, and reason can hardly be satisfied to refer it to any cause which is not superior to itself. So that the idealizing process, so far from supporting the inference that God is only a phantom of our thought, seems rather to suggest an instinctive reaching forth of the rational creature towards the infinite Author of its being.

Having now before our minds the two ideas, the one of God, and the other of man, we are lastly to endeavour, by bringing these into relation to each other, to form an approximate notion of the way in which such a Being, if real and not only ideal, might be expected to become practically known to man.

We have seen that although we cannot justify logically our belief in an external world, or in other human minds, or even in our own personality, yet as a matter of fact we do come to believe in all these with absolute conviction, and upon these beliefs our whole life is practically based. Our instinctive or intuitive consciousness stands in the place of logical proof, and we have no more doubt of its affirmations than we have of the theorems of geometry and mathematics.

The first thought, therefore, which strikes us

is the possibility that God, supposing Him to exist, may become practically known to us in a similar way. Or, to draw out the thought, that environing us as the universe does He may assert Himself in our consciousness, as that asserts itself to be an objective reality ; operating all around us in His infinite intelligence, as our fellow-men do in their finite intelligence, He may be felt by us to be a real Mind, as we feel them to be real minds; and lastly, that pervading our personality as the infinite Source of life and goodness, He may bear in upon us a conviction of His personal existence, analogous to our conviction of our own personality, and may thus become a practically certain, although incomprehensible, Object of knowledge.

From that primary thought we may go on to imagine something of the mode in which such a realization of God, supposing Him to exist, might come about in our consciousness, and frame itself into definite knowledge. Each part of our nature might be expected to be an inlet by which a sense of His Being might enter and take possession of our minds.

First, He might be apprehended by us through onr consciousness of our own efficient, producing will.

Knowing the effects resulting from the action

of our own wills, and observing similar effects produced around us of which we are not the originators, we cannot help ascribing these to like causes, and seeing in them incontrovertible evidence of the exercise of efficient will by our fellow-men. The inference of a producing will in them from the visible phenomena is one which we cannot justify logically, yet we cannot abstain from making it, and we can no more doubt that they are persons who exercise volition and originate effects, than we can doubt of our own existence. But besides the effects which we ascribe to them, we observe others all around us, certainly not due to the human will at all,—the whole congeries of effects which we call Nature, and which we cannot help attributing to some cause, of whatever kind it may be. Now supposing these to be really due to a supreme personal Will, acting with infinitely greater force and wider scope; then we should only be following the hint already given by our experience, if we expected a conviction of the existence and operation of that infinite Will to be borne in on our minds, as we were hourly conversant with the phenomena of Nature. Just as from our fellow-men's works we instinctively, not logically, leaped to the conclusion of their personal operative will; so from habitual observation of God's works in Nature we might expect to find ourselves making a like instinctive leap to His personal existence and action. And conversely, if we did, as a matter of fact, find ourselves doing this instinctively, and referring Nature to a supreme Will as its cause, we should have as much reason to trust this action of our minds, as we had to trust them when they inferred the presence of will in our fellow-men. In both cases the conclusion would rest, not on logical grounds, but on the veracity of our intuitions; and if we accepted it in the one, there seems to be no reason why we should reject it in the other. Hence, through our consciousness of personal will in ourselves, we might expect that God, if really existing, would become practically known to us as the great personal Cause, of whose will the universe is the effect. The corresponding argument for theism is known as the argument from Causation.

Next, the consciousness of our own intelligent faculty may be considered another inlet, through which the knowledge of God, supposing Him to exist, might be expected to reach us.

Purpose and design are facts of our consciousness, and they attest themselves by effects which bear the stamp of intelligence. We adapt and construct, and carry into execution ideas which our minds have conceived, by means which our minds select and employ. Meeting with similar effects which we know were not caused by ourselves, we unhesitatingly attribute them to a similar cause in the intelligence of our fellow-men, and thus arrive at the conclusion that they too have minds as we have. The inference is intuitive or instinctive, and not capable of logical justification. From mechanism we infer mind, because we are conscious of mind in ourselves of which mechanism is the result, and we cannot help assuming that the cases are similar, although strict demonstration of their similarity is impossible.

Well, but Nature also is found to be full of exquisite constructions, adaptations, and organisms, which resemble these works of human intelligence in at least one leading feature, namely, that they display fitnesses of arrangement and collocations of parts conspiring to definite ends. About the original cause of these experience gives us no information. But suppose that they really are the effects of a divine Mind, operating by infinite intelligence in its vaster sphere, as we operate by a finite intelligence in our very limited sphere. Then, judging

from our former experience, we might expect
the inference of an originating Intelligence to
form itself in our minds, as we observed and
examined them, just as a similar inference did in
the case of the handiworks of our fellow-men. In
each case the grounds of the inference would
be the marks of design, interpreted by our
minds in the light of our own conscious possession of designing intelligence; in each case the
inference would be an instinctive one, drawn by
the assumption of an analogy, and lying outside
the limits of any possible demonstration; and if
it was valid in one of the cases, there would appear to be no reason for distrusting it in the
other. Should then this sense or conviction of
a supreme designing Mind be, in actual fact,
forcibly impressed on our minds by the organisms and adaptations abounding in Nature,
that fact would become a witness for the real existence of God. The argument for theism thus
constructed is known as the argument from
Design.

So far the perception of God, supposing Him
to exist and to be apprehended by us, would have
been produced in our minds by means of the pre-
sentation in our consciousness of things external
to ourselves. We have now to look inwards, and
inquire whether from the contemplation of our

own personality a similar result might not be expected to follow.

We have seen that one of the personal elements most clearly revealed in our consciousness is what we call Morality. In proportion to our growth in the true characteristics of humanity, Right, Duty, and Responsibility become words of intense meaning for us. We feel our nature to be under a moral law, not of our own creating, which commands our obedience authoritatively, and avenges our wilful disregard of it by involuntary shame and remorse. Now let us imagine this moral law to be no merely subjective conception, but the expression within us of the will of a real God energizing in our conscience; in that case it would surely appear probable, that a sense of His being and authority would in some way enter into our minds, as we lived and acted under His law. The continual experience of the command, " Thou shalt," and of the prohibition, " Thou shalt not," mysteriously confronting us with an authority to which we could not help bowing in reverence, would naturally, in that case one would think, constrain us to form a conception of a moral Lawgiver under whose rule we were really living. If then, in the actual experience of mankind, the sense of being under a moral law should be found to have given birth almost universally to an instinctive conviction of a supreme Lawgiver, this conviction would be of the nature of a witness for the existence of God. The corresponding argument for theism is known as the argument from the Moral Consciousness.

Once more, we have seen that we are conscious also of a Spiritual element in our personality, the source of our most soaring aspirations, and the seat of our finest affections. By the impulse of this faculty, when developed by cultivation, our desires reach out after an infinite, eternal, all-loving God. Now, if there were indeed such a God, a heavenly Father in whom our hearts could repose, we might reasonably expect that through this faculty He would make Himself felt by us; we might fairly regard it as an inward eye of the spirit given to us by Him expressly that we might see Him with it. Supposing, then, that the more we purged and cultivated this spiritual element of our nature, the more we really felt ourselves to have an inward perception or intuition of God, this experience, although subjective and logically unable to prove the existence of any answering object, would on the same grounds as before be a valid witness for the existence of God. The corresponding argument for theism is known as the argument from the Spiritual Consciousness.

Here then are four distinct inlets through which, if there be a God, it seems antecedently likely that a practical knowledge of His Being would penetrate and take possession of our minds. But to make it quite plain what this hypothetical exposition is aiming at, we will at the risk of a little repetition put the matter in a different way.

Let us now imagine that mankind, while gradually developing themselves through a long course of ages in the arts, sciences, and virtues of civilization, till they had attained the level already reached by the most advanced races in the world, had never at any period of their past history possessed any conception of God, never had the slightest suspicion that such a Being existed; and that then for the first time some teacher arose to declare that there was an eternal, infinite Lord, the maker and ruler of all things, who had all along been governing mankind by a moral law, and was entitled to their cheerful obedience and grateful trust. Would not the world have reason to make some such answer as this? "Impossible! Surely had such a Being been all the while standing to us in so supreme a relation, we must long ago have in some way felt His presence, and become conscious of what He was to us. If this mighty universe sprang into existence by His will, and has been continually upheld by His energy, some thought of this must have been borne in on our minds, as we lived in its midst, and explored its relations and laws. If all this symmetry and beauty, these exquisite organisms and beneficial relations which contribute to our daily use and enjoyment, were really the products of His intelligence, we could not have been observing and using them all these ages without being led to trace His hand in their construction. If our moral nature was of His fashioning, and His will is the supreme law for obedience to which we are responsible, He could not have left our hearts so closed and barred against all knowledge of Him, that not the slightest suspicion of His claim should ever have made its way into them. If we have all along had in Him a loving Father, it is incredible that we should have continued utterly ignorant of the relation, and never enjoyed any opportunity to become sensible of our privilege. We know by ample experience what are will, mind, moral and spiritual affections, and how they manifest themselves; we detect their presence and operation all around us in our fellow-men. It is inconceivable, then, that

we have all along been living as rational and
moral beings, in a world filled with the presence
and works of an infinite Lord and Father,
supreme in power, intelligence, righteousness,
and goodness, and yet up to this hour have never
perceived a trace, never entertained an idea, of
His existence."

The reply, we think, would be unanswerable.
And its force would lie in this, that the four
human attributes of which we have so often
spoken are, by their nature, exactly fitted to let
in on our minds the knowledge of the Supreme
Father, supposing Him really to exist. They
lead us instinctively to recognize our fellow-men's
minds and handiwork; and if they did not lead
on to a similar instinctive recognition of God,
the only reasonable explanation would be that
there was no God to be recognized.

But now, with this thought in our minds, let
us give over feigning an unreal history of mankind, and look back on their actual course. If
we discover the recognition of a supreme Being
to have been as universal as humanity itself, or
at least as humanity in every stage except the
very lowest; if it turns out that a belief in God
as the originating Cause, the designing Intelligence, the moral Lawgiver, and the gracious
Father, has rooted itself everywhere in the hearts

of our race, germinating there as in its native
soil, has ever gained strength with culture of
the best kind, and approved itself with scarcely
a noticeable exception as the goal to which consciousness and experience impel every soul that
loves light and truth; then we shall have found
ample support for our proposition, that belief in
God may rightly be classed among those primary beliefs of the reason which justify themselves by their existence.

There is only one other remark which need
be added here; and it is, that a further confirm-
ation of theism may possibly be found in the
history of its practical working in the world.

Those three great primary beliefs, common to
all men, to which reference has so often been
made, the beliefs in our own Self, the Selves of our
fellow-men, and the physical universe, of which
no logical basis can be predicated, when tried by
the test of their practical working come triumphantly out of the ordeal. On them are built the
entire culture of humanity, the magnificent
structure of science, the domestic, political, and
social relations of mankind. Without them
human life would be impossible. On metaphysical scepticism, however logical, nothing
can be built: in it neither knowledge nor duty
nor love can find a resting-place; it begins and

ends in the mists and phantoms of unreality. I am : my fellow-men are : the universe is : these are the three fundamental articles of the charta of humanity and civilization.

Let belief in God the Father Almighty stand the same test of practical working, and beside this great Triad it may without challenge take its place on equal terms.

CHAPTER V.

THE ARGUMENTS FOR THEISM FROM THE CON-
SCIOUSNESS OF ORIGINATING WILL AND DESIGN-
ING INTELLIGENCE.

Our way to the constructive, or positive, part
of our argument may have seemed long, but we
trust that each step has had its use in clearing
up misunderstandings, removing preliminary
objections, and indicating the direction in which
our search for the true grounds of belief in God
must be finally pursued.

In the first chapter we insisted on the supremacy and universal fruitfulness of the belief in
every province of human thought, emotion, and
conduct; and inferred that the method to be
employed in verifying it, and the field from
which evidence of its truth should be gathered,
must have a proportionate comprehensiveness
and breadth.

In the second chapter we discussed the assertion of the agnostic, that the existence of God

is incapable of proof. That it is incapable of the
kind of proof which is called demonstrative we
confessed; and pointed out that all the suppos-
able methods of demonstration are in their nature
inapplicable, and that their inevitable failure
ought not to prejudice the cause of theism.

In the third chapter we explained the insuf-
ficiency of logical processes to put us in possession of primary truths; and maintained that
inasmuch as all the practical knowledge on
which human life is based comes to us in the
first instance through the perceptions of our
consciousness developed by experience, it is
through the same channel that a practical knowledge of God may be expected to reach us.

In the fourth chapter we endeavoured to ex-
pound the manner in which the method of consciousness may be employed in the search for
God. Inquiring how a sense of God might be
deemed likely to be borne in on our minds,
supposing Him to exist, four different ways
seemed to present themselves; two of them
related to our observation of the external universe, and two to our contemplation of ourselves.
Through viewing the universe as interpreted by
the light of our consciousness of productive will
in ourselves, God might be recognized as its
personal Cause. Through viewing organized

Nature in the light of our consciousness of designing intelligence, God might be apprehended as its intelligent Artificer. Through reflexion on our own moral consciousness might be engendered the conviction of God as the moral Lawgiver. Through contemplation of our own spiritual consciousness God might become known to us as the supreme Father. We then drew the conclusion that if it should appear that these four conceptions of God have not only actually prevailed among mankind and possessed themselves of human thought in general, but also approve themselves to the enlightened reason as being in harmony with its primary intuitions, these facts would furnish valid ground for classing belief in God among those great primary beliefs which justify themselves independently of logical proof.

This is the point at which our discussion now stands; whence it is plain that our task must be to show that those four conceptions of God do actually rise within and take possession of the mind, as ideas which are instinctively felt to have truth and reality beneath them.

We begin by examining the conception which our consciousness of productive will leads us to form of the origination of the universe.

We have already remarked that the better our

H

minds become acquainted with the course of
Nature, the deeper is their conviction that every
event must have had a cause. It may be added
now that the constitution of our minds is such
as to prevent our resting satisfied with tracing
events back to merely physical causes. However
far back we return in the line of causation, our
minds refuse to consider a physical cause as a
true or real cause. Each physical antecedent
requires another to precede it, and that again
another; and as long as we continue in this line
of physical events, each of which is in turn an
effect and a cause, we feel that we have not
reached a real origin. An origin of the series
must lie outside the series; for if it lie within
the series, and be one of its component parts, we
immediately look beyond for a predecessor to it,
and it ceases to be regarded as an origin. The
true origin therefore of every succession of physical causes and effects must lie outside the series,
and within our experience there is nothing which
realizes this condition except an act of Will. A
volition is accepted by our minds as a true origin,
a real cause; but we know of nothing else that
can be placed in the same category. Every
series of physical events which we are able to
trace back to an originating cause runs back
into a volition. Where we cannot arrive at an

originating volition, the series stretches back indefinitely, and so far as we can imagine, for ever. This conception of volition as the only real cause, this refusal to rest in any merely physical antecedent as a true origin, is a primary law of our thought. However it became impressed on our minds, there it certainly is; and when clearly set before us we cannot help thinking in accordance with it.

The imperative character of this law of our thought may be illustrated in this way. A murder is committed by means of fire-arms. What killed the victim? The bullet. Then let us punish the bullet, and have done with the matter. Nonsense! The stroke of the bullet was but a physical antecedent, not a true cause; we must go further back for the criminal. Well then, shall we accuse the gunpowder which impelled the bullet? Nonsense again! How far back then must we go? Shall we fix the guilt on the percussion-cap which ignited the powder; or on the hammer which exploded the cap; or on the spring which forced the hammer to strike; or on the trigger which released the spring; or on the finger which pressed the trigger? Still we are in the series of merely physical antecedents, and we find it impossible to stop at any of them without conscious absurdity, and say,

H 2

"Here is the guilty cause." But what moved the finger? The volition of the human agent. Ah, that is different! Here is the real origin, the true cause. The man is the murderer, because his will set in motion the train of physical causes, at the end of which is the murder. He is the author of the act, and on his head the unanimous verdict of mankind fixes the guilt.

The ineradicable idea of responsibility rests entirely on the conception of volition as the true cause of events. On no other basis can justice be administered, or moral blame or praise be bestowed. Let it be shown that the manslayer exercised no volition in his deed, but was coerced into doing it by superior force, and he is held excused; in that case he was not the cause of the act but only one of its physical antecedents, and the inquiry for the true cause passes beyond him to seek a remoter origin of the transaction. Volition and responsibility are inseparably connected.

Will it be urged in objection that volition itself is not free, but as much necessitated by antecedent causes as physical events are, and is therefore no more a true origin than they are? If that be the case, responsibility is altogether at an end. The crime may be horrible, the judge corrupt, the witnesses perjured, the jury bribed; but it is all necessitated, and blame would be ridiculous. Nay, on the same line of a denial of our primary consciousness, there would be no one to be blamed; criminal and victim, judge and counsel, witnesses and jurymen, would melt away into shadows, and human life and action be dissolved into a dream !

Now in the light of this instinctive belief of our reason, that volition alone really originates, we look out on the universe. We perceive it to be a vast assemblage of physical phenomena of the most complex kind; and when we ask, as our minds impel us to ask, whence they arise, Science attempts to supply the answer. She points back to preceding phenomena, and then to others antecedent to these; and so she leads us back and back, through vast cycles of time, the complexity growing less the farther we recede into the Past, until at last she lands us in a uniform " cosmic vapour." There is her limit. Having reached that, she has done all she can. If we question her farther, she is dumb.

But we are not satisfied. We still ask, Whence this cosmic vapour ? and Science failing us, we look at it in the light of the primary instincts of our reason, and try what we can make of it. Doing so, two alternatives force themselves on our minds for choice; either it was from eternity, or it had a beginning. If it was from eternity, we cannot help thinking that it would never have ceased to be what it was, unless some external power had interfered with it; for if an eternal Past had rolled over it without any change occurring, nothing more could be expected from an eternal Future; all possibilities would already have been exhausted. But as we know that this mysterious vapour did not continue to be a vapour, but at some definite moment began to organize itself into a magnificent cosmos, we are shut up to the conclusion that even were itself eternal some outside power must have taken it in hand, given it the impulse of change, and started it on the new function of organizing itself into a universe of complex being. If, on the other hand, it was not eternal but had a beginning in time, then again some external power must be conceived as originating it. Look then at this primordial vapour as we may, whether we conceive of it as eternal or as beginning in Time, our reason compels us to postulate something else besides it, something which was not it nor any part of it, as the necessary antecedent condition of its having begun to form itself into an organized universe.

The ultimate question, therefore, to which we

are driven back relates to the nature of this something which must have stood, at least outside, if not prior to, the cosmic vapour, to set it agoing on its stupendous function of giving birth to the universe. A physical cause it could not have been; for, in the first place, Science would then have led us beyond the vapour to that antecedent fact, and we should only have had to put our question a step back, and ask, Whence that? and secondly, we have seen that our minds cannot rest in a physical antecedent as a true cause or origin. But if not a physical cause, what then? Science and logic can make no reply; the case is beyond them. But out of our consciousness, developed by experience of life and reality, a clear and unmistakeable answer does come, and that answer is, "A volition." We know of nothing else, can conceive of nothing else, which can really and truly originate a series of physical phenomena. To a volition we are shut up, unless we choose to deny the veracity of consciousness, and accept the alternative of absolute scepticism. But a volition implies a personal Agent; and a personal Agent whose will could start and did start the universe on its course is what we mean by the awful name GOD.

Here then is the goal of the line of thought

on which our consciousness of originating Will launches us. We bring our own experience of Causation into contact with the universe, and we are led straight to the conception of a personal God as its originating cause. As a matter of history, mankind generally in proportion to their light and knowledge have entertained this conviction, and been led instinctively to attribute personality to the power which lies behind the universe. Reflexion shows the conviction to have its roots in the depths of the human consciousness, where all ultimate truths take their rise. Whence we draw the inference that belief in God as the originating Cause of the universe is one of those primary beliefs of the reason which justify themselves.

We go on now to the next branch of our argument, and inquire whether the same rank may not be justly assigned to the conception of God as the intelligent Artificer of Nature.

We called attention some way back to the unquestionable fact, that within the sphere of human activity and experience order, contrivance, and adaptation irresistibly impress us with the conviction that intelligence has been at work in their production. A very slight degree of any of these features is sufficient for the purpose. A Druidicial circle of stones is as

convincing as a Gothic cathedral, a flint arrow-
head from the drift as an inlaid sword-blade
from Damascus. So long as the mechanism or
arrangement or fashioning is of the kind which
we know men to be accustomed to produce, we
draw our inference of intelligent purpose or design with absolute confidence. It rests of course
upon an assumed analogy. We are conscious of
an intelligence in ourselves, by the action of
which such things are produced; we know of
no other cause whatever besides intelligence
which ever originates such things; and hence
whenever we meet with such things, we leap
instinctively to the conclusion that they were
the offspring of minds like our own. So the
habit of inferring mind from the phenomena of
order, contrivance, and adaptation grows upon
us, and roots itself in us as the result of a primary, constitutional tendency or principle of
our thought.

Now that Nature is full of arrangements and
organisms which exhibit, or at least suggest to
our minds, order, contrivance, and adaptation,
no one disputes. Earth and air and sea are
thronged with them. By their complexity,
their delicacy of construction, and fitness for
their peculiar uses or environments, multitudes
of them extort our warmest admiration. The

exquisite mechanism of an eye, an ear, or a hand, is a standing marvel. The world is not a chaos, but a cosmos. Its wonders of harmony, beauty, mutual relation and useful provision, are inexhaustible. If mind be concerned in its production at all, it is manifestly saturated, so to speak, with mind of the highest order, and glows with the light of intelligence throughout all its kingdoms.

All this is beyond question. It is allowed on every side, by believer and sceptic, by theist and atheist, alike. The sole question which arises concerns the originating cause of these countless and elaborate organisms and relations. Are we really compelled to consider them as the off-spring of mind, or can they be satisfactorily accounted for without mind? That in one principal feature they strongly resemble the works of human intelligence is undeniable; for they exhibit that combination of parts and forces conspiring to definite ends, which is the essential characteristic of all Art and Mechanism produced by human hands. But in another respect they as undoubtedly differ from all the works of man. They become, as it were, of themselves; they grow from the germ to maturity by some silent, imperceptible process; whereas the human artificer selects his materials from the substances around him, shapes them and fits them together, and thus by a visible mechanical action brings his constructions to completion. The difference is as obvious as the resemblance; and the question is, whether it so far destroys the analogy as to entitle us to affirm with satisfaction to our reason, that man's works do, and Nature's works do not, constrain us to ascribe them to intelligence.

If it be true that Nature's works do not constrain us to ascribe them to an intelligent cause, it can only be because we perceive some alternative which, if not more satisfactory, is at least as satisfactory to our reason, and does not do violence to the instinctive inferences which are drawn by our consciousness. Let us inquire then what alternatives can be suggested.

There is, it has been urged, a Principle in Nature which determines it to the production of all these things; a principle, that is, which is not mind or intelligence, but works blindly and unconsciously. A slippery thing to get hold of is a principle which exists abstractedly and works of itself, without a mind to entertain and put it in action; but we must do our best in a familiar way to imagine how it may possibly exist and work.

We require some hot water, suppose; and we

hear of a principle which may supply us—a
principle in accordance with which substances
become hot when in contact with fire. Well,
we invoke the principle and await the result.
But we know well by experience that if we do
nothing more, we may wait till the sun itself
has grown cold, and faded out of the sky. If
we want our hot water, we must actively work
the principle ourselves: we must gather the
fuel and kindle it, and put the kettle on, and
keep the fire burning. The abstract principle,
without an intelligent agent to use it, effects
nothing.

Or we want a time-keeper, and we hear of a
principle in accordance with which a steel-
spring, in forcibly uncoiling itself, will turn
wheels at a regulated pace so as to indicate the
lapse of time. We invoke the principle, and
expect our watch. But like the priests calling
on Baal, we shall call and wait in vain. Till
an intelligent workman takes the principle in
hand, makes the spring and the wheels, and
adjusts them so as to produce the required
motion, no watch will come though we wait till
Time expires. The principle alone brings about
nothing.

In fact, try as long as we can to conceive
distinctly of an abstract, unintelligent principle

working effectively of itself, and bringing forth results which resemble the productions of mind, the thing is really unthinkable; reason guided in its judgment by experience is compelled to pronounce the hypothesis of such a principle, as the cause of the exquisite organisms and adaptations of Nature, a collocation of words without intelligible meaning.

But if a Principle will not work, perhaps a Tendency will be more efficient. Things become what they are, it is alleged, in consequence of a tendency to become what they are. The universe is an inexhaustible storehouse of tendency; Nature is the offspring of tendency.

It strikes us at once that if this be a true explanation of natural organisms and relations, there must be a very perplexing number of different and conflicting tendencies. The tendency that produces a crystal cannot originate a flower. The tendency which makes a snail cannot be the same as that which constructs an elephant. There must be at least as many tendencies as there are species of objects in the world; for the original material is common to all. The earths and metals and gases, with all their natural combinations; the countless tribes of the animal kingdom, from whales and mammoths down to the minutest microscopic animalculæ; the equally countless tribes of the vegetable kingdom, from the gigantic conifers to the mosses and lichens and floating organisms of the air; every one of these, it would seem, must have had its appropriate tendency, without the action of which it could not have come into being. What an amazing host of tendencies, "thick as autumnal leaves that strew the brooks in Vallombrosa," all energizing and striving without a moment's intermission in the whole realm of Nature! Think of a single atom of matter fought over by thousands of rival tendencies, each struggling to impress itself on the inert substance; and then imagine a like battle waged over every atom which exists in the broad earth and circumambient air and star-strewn heavens. What confusion worse confounded! What eternal anarchy and chaos! And this is the account which reason is sometimes asked to prefer to the supposition of a presiding mind, of the origin of all the manifold symmetry, variety, and loveliness of our wonderful and glorious universe. Truly may every rational instinct in us cry out in vociferous protest against the substitution of blind tendency for God.

But a more stately hypothesis now advances on the scene. We are summoned to do homage to cosmic evolution, as the complete solution of the problem of existence.

"Look," we are told, "at one of the great natural organisms, and recollect how it has developed itself from a simple microscopic cell till it stands before you in mature and manifold perfection. Out of the germ of the oak-blossom watch the mighty tree unfolding itself, by an automatic progress, into a massive trunk anchored in the soil by roots which defy the storm, huge branching limbs ramifying into hundreds of boughs and thousands of twigs, and these clothed with a wealth of thick foliage beneath whose shade a whole flock may repose, and bearing myriads of blossoms and seeds in their season. Observe the minute ovum of the vast pachydermatous mammal pursuing a like course of development, till the huge creature, strong in bone and sinew, and perfect in each various organ, limb, and sense, stands before you a living, breathing, multiform whole. Enlarge the idea thus acquired, and see how well it fits the great All. In the primeval cosmic cloud to which Science takes you back, you behold the original germ or ovum of the universe. Thence unfolding itself by its own laws it grew and waxed great, ever evolving new combinations, giving birth to higher

organisms, becoming more varied and complex,
richer in beauty and intelligence, till the hour
when you yourself were cradled on its bosom,
one of the countless myriads of myriads of its
offspring. Thus the mystery of being is solved.
The law of existence is automatic evolution."

A stately theory, we must confess, and one
which gives the fullest expression to that sense
of unity which arises from an intelligent contemplation of the universe. With a single
addition reason perhaps might gladly welcome
it. But here, as in many other things, the
first step is the difficulty. We stumble at the
outset, and are at a loss to understand how the
evolution gets itself into motion. Given the
germ, and all goes smoothly. But of a germ
which exists of itself without derivation from
any living parent we have absolutely no experience. The cosmic cloud which evolution
postulates must surely have been instinct with
the most various and amazing powers and
properties. Every kind of being must be conceived to have been potentially contained in it;
all worlds and all their contents; all orders of
life, animal and vegetable; all the elements of
the intellectual and moral faculties of mankind,
and of every other race of rational beings; all
that makes the genius, the hero, the philosopher,

and the saint. All contained in the particles of that primeval cloud, together with the stupendous faculty of constructing out of the diffused material every individual existence that has ever passed across the crowded stage of Time. For, according to the hypothesis, this wondrous germ-cloud was the artificer as well as the material, the artist as well as the vehicle of his skill. The collocation of the parts of every eye, ear, and hand was as much due to it as the substance out of which they are made; life, thought, conscience, as much as the material particles of the brain and nerves. It was the All potentially, and from it by its own inherent forces and properties the All has been evolved.

Now here is our difficulty, when it is proposed to us to accept this substitute for God. The theory suggests no means of getting this amazing, elaborate universe-germ, to start the majestic Evolution on its course. Nothing has as yet been accounted for; the origination of all the organisms and adaptations of Nature has still to be sought. The great question of a primal cause has only been put back, not solved. It faces us when we have gone back to the cosmic cloud, just as much as it did in the matured objects of our admiration. If we could have gone one step farther back, and discerned behind

I

the primeval nebulousness a mighty Intelligence which first ideally designed the universe, and then endowed the germ-cloud with such substance and properties as were sufficient to enable it to realize the design, our reason would have been satisfied; we should have bowed the head in reverence, and confessed the supreme Mind of which Nature is the glorious handiwork. But this is what the theory does not permit. Its object is to show that God is unnecessary; to explain the universe without Him. It binds us down to Evolution without a cause, without an intelligence; and thereby leaves it hanging in the air without support. We ask for an agent, and it puts us off with a mode of action. We inquire for a true origin of an exquisite piece of workmanship, and it shows us the work already in progress and there abandons us. Our reason therefore cannot but protest that the solution of the mystery of the universe offered by cosmic Evolution is insufficient, and leaves the secret absolutely untold.

We have been seeking an alternative for Mind, by which the harmoniously ordered and elaborately constructed system of Nature might reasonably be supposed to have been fashioned. And we have failed. Unintelligent principle, inherent tendency, cosmic evolution, have in

turn offered themselves, but reason compels us
to reject them as inadequate ; they are unwork-
able as theories, unthinkable as ultimate causes.
We are therefore thrown back on Mind; and
we are thrown back on it by that instinctive
sense of the necessity of things, which, however
we got it, whether it was born with us, or acquired by experience, has become rooted in us as
part of our mental structure.   We cannot bring
ourselves to think that this magnificent universe
was uncaused.   We may indeed put that proposition into words, and spin webs of argument
about it ingenious enough to bewilder ourselves
and others ; but as soon as we try honestly to
grapple with the idea, and drag it face to face
with our practical reason, it eludes us and
vanishes like a spectre of darkness at cockcrow.
Caused the universe must have been, we are
sure.   But how ?   When we have tracked it
back to the cosmic vapour of Science, we have
only watched a process, not reached an origin.
That too, we are sure, must have been caused.
But the cause of that, the primordial cause, antecedent to the whole physical evolution, is it
absolutely unknowable and inscrutable, or are we
justified in calling it Mind ?

  That is the final question, and the answer to
it comes, not from our logical faculty, which for.

want of materials for demonstration is unable to
help us here, but from our intuitive consciousness. From this springs the clear, unhesitating
reply, " The cause must be Mind." For it is
not an eternal chaos, a drear waste of unchang-
ing, stagnant, formless matter, that we are contemplating ; but a growing, progressive cosmos,
an unfolding universe of harmony and order,
teeming with adaptation and contrivance,
mechanism and adjustment. Of such things we
cannot think without being impressed with the
idea of design, nor even speak without employ-
ing language which implies intention and purpose. Who really doubts, except it be under
the stress of some rigorous and tyrannical theory,
that the eye was intended for seeing, the lung
for breathing, the fins for swimming, the mater-
nal instinct for rearing progeny ?   Or who can
avoid using such language without being conscious of a pedantic and unnatural self-restraint?
We know that within our own sphere of action
mind, and mind alone, originates contrivances,
adjustments, mechanisms, relations of use and
beauty.   Of any other cause which can originate such things here or elsewhere we are as
ignorant, and even as unable to conceive, as of
a new bodily sense, or of a world where two
straight lines can enclose a space.   And thus

the conviction grows up within us, as a primary
or instinctive belief of the reason, that order,
contrivance, and adaptation indicate the action
of intelligence; and from the contemplation of
such phenomena we spring, and human reason
has always sprung, to the conception of an originating Mind.

Here, then, is the goal to which the consciousness of designing intelligence brings us, and
has brought the world in general, when contemplating the order and mechanism of Nature.
It is a Supreme Mind as the Artificer of the
universe.   But that again is what we mean by
the awful name GOD.

The continuance of the inquiry along the
two lines of consciousness which still remain to
be examined must be reserved for the two following chapters.

CHAPTER VI.

THE ARGUMENT FOR THEISM FROM THE MORAL
CONSCIOUSNESS.

THE discussion on which we now enter differs in a considerable degree from those which occupied the preceding chapter. For them we obtained the materials from outside our own personality, by observation of the external universe; now it is the Self within which we contemplate, and from which we shall endeavour to ascend to God.

In this chapter the moral element of our being is to be interrogated, to ascertain if it bears witness to a supreme Lawgiver. Of course, to the mere logician, bent on weaving demonstrations by syllogistic processes out of axiomatic premisses, our moral nature is a purely subjective thing, from which nothing external to itself can be legitimately inferred. But to us who are looking for those primary instinctive or intuitive beliefs which underlie all possible logical proof,

the real question is whether, as a matter of fact
and human experience, the consciousness of a
moral nature does not beget the conviction of an
objective moral law and a supreme Lawgiver.

Right and Wrong, are they truly irreconcileable extremes?   Do they confront each other
eternally at opposite poles of rational existence?
Whatever speculative philosophers may argue,
to these questions the great heart of humanity
returns an unwavering reply in the affirmative.
There is no language in which the word "ought"
is destitute of a solemn meaning, or the word
"duty" has ceased to carry with it a sacred imperative.   Never has there been a society constructed on the principle that moral differences
are mere figments of the imagination, or products
of custom and fashion; never a religion which
dispensed with a distinction between moral good
and evil.   If ever there have existed individual
human beings, who d`nied their possession of
any faculty which witnessed for right and pro-
tested against wrong, they are held by the
general verdict of the race to have been but dis-
torted and monstrous specimens, in whom the
noblest element of humanity was deficient.

Concurrently with the conviction of an eternal, irreconcileable opposition between Right and
Wrong, there has always existed in the human

breast a sense of responsibility. The moral judgment carries with it a felt authority and sanction.
It differs essentially from the judgments of the
intellect, in having self-approval and shame for
its ministers. When it has pronounced on the
rightness of an action in the existing circumstances, we feel that we are summoned to perform
that action. We cannot put the decision aside
as one with which we have no practical concern;
it haunts us, it presses on us, it demands our
obedience; and if we refuse to obey, we experience a sensation of uneasiness, self-reproach,
and shame. Hence arises the consciousness of
responsibility. When we know what is right,
we cannot help feeling accountable for neglecting to do it; whatever ill consequences follow
from our disobedience to the sacred voice within,
we recognize that they are justly chargeable
upon us; we cannot repudiate them; responsibility
for them is a burden from which there is no
release.

Nor is that all. The sense of responsibility
irresistibly forces on us the idea of a tribunal at
which we must answer, an objective moral law
which lies upon us and is armed with retributive
sanctions. The history of all nations shows that
the human mind has never been able to restrict
the idea of moral responsibility to a purely sub-

jective conception; the advance to an external
authority, commanding, and enforcing its commands, has been found inevitable, and is thus
evinced to be rooted in the constitution of our
nature—in other words, to be instinctive. In
whatever form the conception has embodied
itself; whether of a Nemesis that dogs the heels
of guilt, or a Tendency that works in favour of
virtue, or an " Eternal not-ourselves that makes
for righteousness," or a Judge at whose bar the
disembodied soul is arraigned after death, or a
supreme moral Governor of the universe; the
substance of it has been that there really is
outside us, and independent of us, a moral law
under which we live, and an administration of
justice which somehow, whether in this or a
future life, or in both, takes cognizance of
human actions and is armed with the power
of retribution. The law within the breast has
always been more or less distinctly regarded as
the reflection of a law which is outside and
above; the voice of conscience within as the echo
of a sovereign voice without; the sense of
guilt and shame as the shadow of an avenging
Power, to which moral agents are accountable
for their deeds.

All this is plain matter of fact, independent
of any speculations as to its origin or significance.

An ineradicable sense of the antagonism between Right and Wrong, and of human responsibility, giving birth to the conception of an external Moral Law and Tribunal of Justice, is a primary fact of human nature.

Doubtless it is very possible to put this fact into the alembic of critical analysis, and resolve it into its supposed elements, till all that is significant in it seems to disappear, and nothing worth noting is left behind. There are no moral or spiritual facts which may not be got rid of in this way, and the process may easily be continued till human nature is stripped of everything that honourably distinguishes it from the beasts of rapine.

Mankind have only to be portrayed in an imaginary primitive condition, just emerging from the bestial stage, and beginning to live in rude communities, ignorant of everything but how to provide a scanty sustenance for their bodily life. Moral distinctions would at first be as foreign to them as to tigers and rattlesnakes. But some actions would soon be found to promote the well-being of the nascent tribe, others to be adverse to it; and accordingly the former would be approved and rewarded, the latter censured and punished. Then the word Right would be invented to describe those, the word Wrong these. So as time ran on, and succeeding generations inherited the gradually accumulated experience of their forefathers, ideas of rightness and wrongness would be formed, and grow into force and completeness; virtue would mean what benefited the social life, vice what harmed it; and thus the whole genesis of morality, conscience, responsibility, awe of a supreme moral Power, would be accounted for as easily and thoroughly as the art of building houses or weaving cloths.

But as soon as we come back from such excursions into an imaginary Past, and bring the conclusions which we have gathered there into the still and awful chamber of our moral consciousness, we discover an irreconcileable antagonism. When we hear the solemn voice within say to us, " Thou shalt not," it surely is not the fear of disapproval by the social body which is dissuading us from the action. When shame and self-reproach crimson the cheek in secret, and the voice within pronounces, " Thou art verily guilty," it surely is not an anticipation that the community will blame us for neglecting its interests. When the heart is ennobled by a consciousness of rectitude and harmony with the eternal law of Right, the feeling is surely something more than an expectation that our fellow-citizens will deem our conduct advantageous to the commonwealth. When the tempted soul contentedly renounces its dearest earthly hopes, and the martyr goes cheerfully to his baptism of blood, rather than incur a stain of dishonour or unfaithfulness, it surely is no mere echo of social law which rises into such commanding authority over the strongest desires of our nature. When the human spirit bows down in self-abasing reverence before One who is infinite righteousness and truth, it surely is not to the idealized opinion of society that the worship is offered.

A thousand times, no! The whole moral nature within us protests against such a lowering of its significance, such a degradation of its essential character and proper dignity. Experience and culture may have contributed to unfold it, in its passage downwards from the ruder primitive times; just as in each individual now it grows from weakness and indistinctness in the child to the maturity of its powers in the man. But for its origin no experience nor culture can reasonably account. Cultivation unfolds germs, it does not create them; without the germ to start with, it effects nothing.

The vast difference in kind between moral sensations and all others cannot be too closely observed, if we would comprehend the real nature of morality. Let any one who doubts the fundamental nature of the distinction carefully pass under review the various sources of pleasurable sensations of which he has any knowledge. Let him begin with observing the keenest gratifications of the senses; let him go on to the intellectual pleasures of science, imagination, art; let him explore the delights of gratified ambition, social success, prosperous endeavour; let him bring under examination the happiness arising from satisfied affection and domestic tranquillity; in a word, let him take account of every kind of enjoyment of which man is capable, except that which springs directly from a moral source: and between all those, and this one excepted delight, he will find an absolutely impassable gulf. Those are enjoyments, pleasures, delightful sensations, which brighten life while they last, and perhaps for a time will yield a faint fragrance in the memory; and when that is said of them all is said. But the joy of having done a good deed, conquered a base passion, made a cheerful sacrifice of self in unselfish love, is as much higher and purer as heaven is higher and purer than earth; this ennobles as well as gratifies; this is a joy for ever, victorious over time and destiny.

Or let him take the reverse side. Physical discomfort and pain, disappointments of ambition or affection, the deprivation of mental gratifications, are often hard to bear, and extort many a groan from suffering humanity. But can any one with the smallest show of reason weigh them in the scale against the stings of avenging conscience, the self-contempt and shame which spring from wilful wrong-doing, the remorse which burns into the memory the agonizing sense of guilt? Ah! these are causes of suffering which are separated from all the rest by a whole diameter of the soul; these unnerve and poison and torture the heart; for these earth has no medicament, time brings no cure.

That there is, then, in human nature a distinct and imperial moral faculty we cannot doubt. It proclaims itself in our moral judgments; it speaks authoritatively in the voice of our conscience; it charges home on us the responsibility of our actions; it lashes our disobedience with the scourges of shame and remorse; it raises before us dread visions of retribution. Over our entire personality it claims rightful and supreme rule, and sits enthroned as a lawful sovereign in the midst of our various appetites, passions, and powers.

That this mysterious and sacred inmate of our

breasts has in all ages led mankind to believe in an external reality corresponding to it, namely, in an objective moral law, and a supreme Power which enforces it, is, as we have already observed, an undeniable fact of history. For our present purpose the value of the fact lies in this, that it leads us to view this inference as being of the nature of a primary intuition of the reason. For if it be so, it becomes a valid witness for the existence of God.

There are, however, several considerations which may be added to the historical fact, as further evidence that this great inference from the moral consciousness is really entitled to the character of a primary, instinctive belief. These, then, we proceed to set forth.

The first is, the impossibility of accounting for this moral element in human nature, except by the supposition of a righteous Lawgiver who planted it there as a witness to Himself.

To say that it came of itself, or is the result of a particular configuration of the particles of the brain, is merely to evade the question by using phrases which really have no meaning. Nothing comes of itself; and if any one persuades himself that he is able to conceive of particles of the brain, or any other particles, originating righteousness, truth, purity, and

love, we-can only leave him alone in the enjoyment of so singular a faculty.

Equally beside the purpose is the explanation which ascribes the moral faculty to the
accumulated and transmitted experience of
what makes for the welfare of the community.
We have already seen with what vehemence our
moral consciousness protests against any such
account of the genesis of morality, as being
ludicrously inadequate, and leading to results in
glaring antagonism to those which flow from
the high and sacred element enthroned in our
breasts.

Nor will the splendid theory of cosmic Evolution help us here. It has already failed to yield
us the faintest clue to the real origin of any
animal or even vegetable organism ; much less
does it explain how the ineradicable sense of
Right and Wrong was engendered, or show how
the atoms of a whirling cloud could possibly
have been transmuted into the heroism of
Duty, the aspiration after Purity, or the passionate thirst for Truth.

Yet morality is a fact, a transcendent fact,
rooted in the very depths of our nature, and
filling our minds with awe at the grandeur and
sacredness of its presence. We cannot help
asking whence it came, and what it means ; and

from one quarter only can we conceive of an answer being returned in which reason can rest contented.

If we might be allowed to imagine a Being of infinite righteousness whose creatures we are, and who has placed this faculty in us as a witness to Himself, and to make us capable of being the subjects of His moral rule, then everything connected with our consciousness of morality would be amply explained. The faculty would be His gift, conscience His voice within us, the moral law His law, responsibility the shadow of His authority over us, retribution His righteous judgment.

Here, then, we are in the presence of a conjunction of particulars which merits our closest attention. First, a grand elementary fact of our humanity; secondly, one and only one conceivable way of satisfactorily accounting for it, but that way entirely and absolutely sufficient; and lastly, an instinctive acceptance of that explanation as to the true one by mankind generally, in proportion as the development of their faculties has enabled them to reflect upon and interpret the phenomena of their moral consciousness.

If such a combination of particulars does not entitle the belief in an objective moral law, and

K

a supreme Lawgiver by whom it is enforced, to be reckoned among the primary beliefs of human reason, to discover any such beliefs would seem to be impracticable.

Our next consideration is the extreme difficulty of justifying the sense of responsibility, except by referring it to a sovereign Authority to whom we are accountable.

If we examine this element of our consciousness, as manifested in our experience, we soon discover that the feeling of responsibility can be directed towards persons alone, and cannot be drawn out towards impersonal things. To say that we owe a duty to a physical law would be an abuse of language. If I thrust my hand heedlessly into a fire, I am burnt and must suffer; but to say that I have broken a moral obligation towards the fire would be absurd. If I wantonly and in mischief cut down a noble tree, whatever blame may attach justly to me certainly does not arise from my having failed in any moral duty which I can owe to the tree. Moral responsibility, as it is a feeling which can arise in none but persons, so also it can be felt towards none but persons.

Who then are the objects of it? To whom does this imperious, haunting feeling of responsibility reach out and refer?

Let us try the first answer that occurs,—Ourselves. Is it really to the Self within that each of us feels that solemn and awful sense of being answerable? If so, we must imagine ourselves resolved each into a double self, one which feels the responsibility, and the other towards which the responsibility is felt. The latter self must be regarded by the former as a separate entity outside itself, clothed with authority and empowered to exact the fulfilment of duty. Looking at this self, the other or acting self must feel itself bound to it by obligations, for the breach of which it is answerable. Of this complex conception of responsibility the inevitable effect would be to reduce the entire action of the solemn feeling to a private matter, confined within the individual breast and operative only at the caprice of the individual. To be responsible to myself is like owing a debt to myself. It has no significance. If I owe it, I am none the more liable; if I pay it, I am none the richer or poorer. The whole conception is imaginary; the distinction is verbal, the consequence nugatory.

Are our fellow-men, then, the persons to whom we are responsible? There is, of course, a sense and a degree in which the feeling finds its object in them. We may enter into relations with

them which create a real responsibility. Whoever
voluntarily accepts employment from another,
and covenants to render him faithful service,
becomes answerable to him for his conduct. Responsible government is government by persons
to whom the country entrusts the task, and who
of their free choice undertake it, and are therefore
responsible to the country for their administration.
The responsibility of man to man springs out of
voluntary engagements. If they are broken,
the person who fails in performance feels that
the sufferer has a right to complain, and to exact
compensation or inflict proportionate punish-
ment. That is all. Of responsibility strictly
limited to our fellow-men, and indebted for its
sanction and force to no other source than our
relations to them, this is the only account which
can be given.

But it is obvious that this does not at all
accord with the consciousness of responsibility
as it is known to us by experience. If the whole
accountability of man arises from a voluntary
engagement to his fellow-man, then the wilful
and base betrayer of a trust, as soon as he has
either made compensation or taken his punish-
ment, might dismiss the transaction from his
memory, and think none the worse of himself.
The responsibility would be discharged and done

with. But the fact is terribly otherwise. He bears to his grave the crushing sense of responsibility. His turpitude haunts him, abases him, fills him with a sense of unworthiness, stings him with remorse. This surely is something very different from the feeling that his fellow-man has a right to complain of his failure to fulfil a contract.

Perhaps it will be said that the feeling of having offended against a moral law is what creates the shame and self-reproach. Most true; but what does this mean? If the moral law were purely subjective, a rule of conduct without extrinsic force, and existing nowhere but in the individual's mind, the obligation to obey it would simply be an obligation to himself, and of such an obligation the practical effect, as we have already seen, would be nugatory. If, on the other hand, the law were really objective and had force and reality independently of the individual's mind, still as long as it remained impersonal, even if we could conceive of such a thing as an impersonal obligatory law, it could not evoke any real sense of responsibility, for it is only to persons that we can feel that sense of obligation out of which responsibility emerges. So that the explanation, to be satisfactory, must bring us round to the conception of a Person above us, to whom we are accountable, and whose will expresses and enforces the eternal law of morality.

No one can doubt that this conception, if it could be entertained, would supply a full and adequate reason for that urgent and haunting sense of responsibility which clings to us like our shadow. If indeed there be a holy God who created us moral beings, and rules us by moral law, the natural and appropriate response of our hearts to that tremendous reality is an ineradicable and dominant conviction that to Him we must give account. And inasmuch as mankind have been led by reflection on, or at any rate by the working of, their consciousness of responsibility to entertain this conception, we argue that it really is a genuine product of their mental constitution, and therefore that belief in a supreme moral Governor may justly be ranked among the primary beliefs of the reason.

There is still another consideration to be added, which is, that the practical working of the moral faculty cannot be satisfactorily explained without reference to the will of a supreme Lawgiver.

It is certain that the moral faculty is capable of working efficiently, and on the whole does work in the world with very considerable effect. If it did not mankind would be savages, and all

the sweetness and grace of human life would be
unknown. Whatever is venerable and pure,
honest and true, lovely and of good report among
the children of men is the fruit and the witness
of its energy. In some quarters, especially in
alliance with the religious sentiment, we see it
rise to a height and a glory which win from our
hearts their most reverential and enthusiastic
homage. Saintly men and women have kept
their purity unstained amidst the most fascinat-
ing allurements of vice; have bridled in every
headstrong passion and rampant ambition, and
trodden with unfaltering steadfastness the toil-
some paths of duty; have sacrificed their own
ease, comfort, hopes, life itself, for the sake of
alleviating suffering, rescuing the perishing,
raising the fallen. On tens of thousands of
spiritual battle-fields has self been vanquished,
and the sacred affection of Love been throned as
a queen, to whom obedience has been ungrudg-
ingly rendered by every energy and passion of
the soul. It is only by these its noblest triumphs
that the working of the moral faculty can be
adequately judged.

Now whence does the faculty derive the almost
superhuman power to rise to these heights of
heroism and nobleness?

There are three leading theories of morality

expounded by systematic writers on ethics, each of which must be questioned to see if it can supply a reasonable answer.

According to the first, which has received the uncouth name of HEDONISM, or the science of pleasure, the rule of conduct is the maxim of doing always what will yield one's self the greatest total amount of gratification. If what is called Virtue seems on the whole to yield more pleasure than Vice, then the follower of this rule will aim at practising Virtue. But as he would do it for his own advantage, and simply for what he could get by it, he could scarcely expect the common sense of mankind to credit him with morality at all. At any rate, to look to the principle of securing at all costs the greatest possible amount of one's own gratification for moral heroisms and noble sacrifices, would be at least as absurd as to expect grapes from brambles and figs from thistles.

According to the second theory of ethics, commonly called UTILITARIANISM, and sometimes ALTRUISM, the rule of conduct is the maxim of doing always that which will produce the greatest happiness to the greatest number of persons. A system, truly, of the purest benevolence, to which no taint of selfishness can be attributed; but our question is whether it contains within

itself the force to make it work. Suppose a
person to say, " I perceive that my denying myself this or that gratification, or my voluntary
subjection of myself to this or that suffering,
would produce more happiness for others than
would arise from my indulging or sparing myself. But what I do not see is why I should on
that account deny or sacrifice myself. My own
happiness is surely a much nearer and more
important concern to me than the happiness of
any one else can possibly be, and consequently
has a far stronger claim on my attention; and
it seems to me that to throw it away for the
sake of others would be an act contrary to
the common sense on which I pride myself, and
worthy only of irrational enthusiasts." Suppose
a person to argue in that way, what reply could
the Utilitarian theory furnish? Absolutely
none! It is an excellent rule of practice, but
of moving force it has not a shadow.

According to the third theory of Ethics, distinguished as the INTUITIONAL, the rule of conduct
is the maxim of always obeying the intuitive
sense of right which dwells in every human
breast. An admirable principle indeed, though
perhaps involving some serious difficulties in
the use of it as a guide amidst the complex circumstances of human life. But what concerns

us now is not the adequacy of the rule, but the
provision of a motive strong enough to make it
work. Let us suppose that a choice must be
made between the alternatives of sinning and
suffering. In one shape or other a choice of
this kind is continually being forced on human
beings; their lives are beset with temptations
from one end to the other, and the force of every
temptation lies in the apparent gain attainable
by wrongdoing. Let us suppose the temptation
presented in the most emphatic shape: "Sin,
and live to enjoy; refuse to sin, and perish;"
and as before, let us ask what reply the theory
will enable the sorely-tried soul to give. "I
know it is nobler to die rather than sin," the
wavering man may answer; "the intrinsic superiority of obeying the voice of conscience at all
hazards is attested unmistakeably by my consciousness. But life is a practical matter, not a
theory or idea. Is it really better for me to keep
my conscience unstained, and thereby perish in
my integrity; or by doing an act which conscience condemns, to preserve my life with all
its opportunities of action and enjoyment? The
beneficial consequences of the wrongdoing are
plain and undeniable; but of any gain to be
secured by dying in my integrity my intuition
tells me nothing. On that side all is blank.

Suffering virtue is doubtless admirable in imagination; but till I am assured of some compensating future which awaits it, common sense forbids me to sacrifice the substance for the shadow." That the reply would be an ignoble one may be admitted; but the logic of it would be unquestionable. Not even by the Intuitive theory of Ethics is a sufficient working force of morality supplied.

Yet morality has ever worked, and continues to work; its triumphs are the glory of human nature. Whence then does it fetch that motive force, of which none of the theories can give an explanation?

Not from earth, but from heaven. The soul springs up from its own moral consciousness to the conception of an infinitely righteous Will, supreme over all things, and sure to bring about a final coincidence of well-being with well-doing. Instinctive belief in a holy God solves the difficulty and supplies the force. Assume His existence and rule, and the inference is inevitable that it must go well with the righteous. Sufferers for conscience sake have the Lord of the universe on their side. Ignominy, privation, torture, death itself, may be their lot here; but they can afford to smile at their losses, as they "commit the keeping of their souls to Him

in well-doing, as unto a faithful Creator."
(1 Pet. iv. 19.)

It is time now to sum up the reply of the
moral faculty to our interrogation of it respecting its witness to the existence of God. ,

We have observed the uniqueness and grandeur of the faculty, existing in man as an essential part of his constitution, and manifesting
itself in a recognition of the eternal distinction
between Right and Wrong, in the voice of conscience, the sense of responsibility, the passion
of remorse, and the fear of retribution.

We have further noticed that in all ages and
among all nations, in proportion to men's growth
and culture in the higher attributes of humanity,
this faculty has led them to the conception of an
objective moral law under which they were
placed, and of a supreme moral Governor to
whom they were accountable.

Once more, we have seen that while this conception affords an adequate explanation of the
origin of the faculty, of the sense of responsibility
to which it gives birth, and of the force by which
it wins its practical triumphs, of these great
facts of human nature reason discovers no other
solution which can be pronounced adequate.

Here then we find ourselves in face of a belief
in a supreme righteous Lawgiver, characterized

by these three features : it has its roots in one of the noblest elements of human nature; it has sprung up, with scarce an exception, wherever any tolerable degree of civilization has prevailed ; and it is shown by reflection to be in entire harmony with the demands of reason. But such a Lawgiver is what we mean by the awful name GOD.

The conclusion seems inevitable that belief in God, as the supreme Lawgiver to whom we are responsible, is really one of those primary, intuitive beliefs which justify themselves by their existence.

CHAPTER VII.

THE ARGUMENT FOR THEISM FROM THE SPIRITUAL CONSCIOUSNESS.

WE have arrived now at the last division of our
constructive argument, and it remains to question that spiritual element of which we are conscious in ourselves, whether it has any trustworthy testimony to bear to the existence of
God. This is the crowning part of our inquiry,
and to do it justice requires a peculiarly candid
and delicate appreciation of facts, which lie the
most remote from those which can be dealt with
by physical or logical processes.

The nature of the spiritual faculty in man has
already been briefly indicated. There are aspirations in us which stretch forth towards the
infinite; affections which transcend calculation;
religious emotions which struggle to pour themselves out to a supreme Personality in boundless
adoration, self-abasement, trust, self-sacrifice,
and love. These are the signs and witnesses of

this soaring faculty, the actings by which its existence and nature are revealed.

That these point to a real and definite element of our personality seems unquestionable. With neither our animal instincts nor our logical understanding have they anything in common ; nor can they be, without violence to facts, identified even with the action of our moral faculty. For the facts of consciousness to which this latter endowment of our being gives birth, the perception of right, the authority of conscience, the sense of duty and responsibility, the satisfaction derived from conscious integrity, although they may often appear to emerge within the peculiar sphere of spiritual feeling, and be almost inextricably intertwined with the more vivid emotions kindled by the religious sentiment, yet in themselves differ essentially from those in which the spiritual faculty displays its characteristic properties. The grave conviction of the distinction between moral good and evil, is easily to be distinguished from that passionate protest against wrong, that boundless aspiration after justice, to which the panting soul, aflame with a divine indignation, strives in vain to give adequate utterance. A moral approbation of the golden rule, to do as we would be done by, cannot be confounded with the impassioned

love which overleaps every limitation, loses all
thought of self, and struggles to exhaust itself
in nothing short of utter self-abandonment and
immolation. The reverential submission of the
will to the supreme Ruler and Judge is a feeling that lies a long way apart from those fervent
religious emotions of which the human spirit is
conscious towards the supreme Goodness, and
which can only utter themselves inarticulately
in ecstasies of gratitude and love, worship and
praise. It is the spiritual element in man which
kindles morality into a burning aspiration for
unsullied purity and unbounded perfection, im-
pels the soul towards the infinite and eternal,
and both craves and finds in God the object of
its affections and hopes, its centre of repose and
its everlasting portion.

Now, when this faculty falls into the hands
of the hostile analyst, it may easily share the
fate which we saw befall the moral consciousness, and like that seem to evaporate and disappear in the crucible of critical examination.
And all the more readily because of its more
etherial texture, and its operation being in a
sphere which lies more out of the way of busy
social life. A great solvent of it is found in the
idealizing faculty, and by a free use of this the
process of disintegrating all that is spiritual in

human nature goes on with marvellous ease and success, till a bare residuum of gross and earthly material is all that is left behind.

Primitive tribes, we are told, emerging from the bestial condition of their ancestors, gradually acquired the feelings and affections which are characteristic of mankind in their riper state of culture and social development; and when they had reached a stage of growth at which they were relieved from the overwhelming pressure of material wants, the imagination found leisure to exercise itself on those feelings and affections, to idealize their elements and feign more elevated objects for them; and thus, out of these lower materials there grew up a romance of spiritual relationship, religious emotion and worship. But touch the result, it is added, with that magic wand of criticism, which like Ithuriel's spear unmasks disguise and makes the homely reality of things apparent, and the stately structure which seemed to tower towards heaven dissolves into an exhalation, and leaves nothing behind but the familiar affections and relations of our earthly state.

Now, we do not doubt that to persons in whom the religious sentiment is dormant and inoperative, an explanation of this kind of the genesis of spiritual feeling may seem plausible,

L

perhaps even convincing. Unconscious themselves of any yearnings after God, any soaring
away of the heart to find elevation and repose
in a Being of infinite goodness, it may appear
reasonable to them to think that such feelings,
when alleged to exist in others, are fanciful,
morbid, or even hypocritical. No argument can
be too flimsy, no explanation too meagre, to
dispose satisfactorily of even the plainest facts
in the estimation of persons who possess no
faculty for understanding them. What are the
glories of the flushing dawn or the tender sunset
to eyes which are sightless? What the rapture
of sweet melodies to ears to which hearing has
been denied? What the fine scruples of delicate
honour to minds which are coarse and treacher-
ous? What the exquisite joy of self-devoting
affection to hearts which are steeped in selfishness? And if the eyes know nothing of that
far-away look which searches restlessly for God;
if the ears have never listened in the still soli-
tude with a tremulous longing, to catch some
whisper of His voice; if the heart has never
sighed to be delivered from its own impurity, by
being bathed in the cleansing flood of His goodness, and has never burned with desire to offer
itself up to Him a living sacrifice; how easy it is
to look down on such experiences with a smile of

superior knowledge, and be satisfied that they have no basis in reality, and are merely fantastic forms which the commonplace relations of social life assume, when brooded over by minds addicted to ideality and dreaming reverie!

But to those who know by experience what religion is, whose souls are on fire with a passionate longing for God, and are thrilled with the joy of communion with Him in His goodness and love, it is really impossible that any explanation of this kind should fail to appear infected with the taint of egregious absurdity and baselessness. What, while they are feeling God within themselves as the un-failing source of their strength and peace and hope; while they are perceiving Him by a spiritual intuition as vividly as their eyes discern the brightness of the sun, or their ears hear the deep roll of the thunder; while He is more real to them than even friend, or child, or wife, and their whole being so centres consciously in Him and reposes upon Him, that to snatch Him from them would leave a void and a desolation in their hearts, more drear and dark than if the world were blotted out around them : to tell these God-seeing, God-filled souls with a jaunty air that all this is but a baseless dream, and they are but weaving webs of idle fancies, and

constructing a romance of the imagination by
idealizing the ordinary relations of social life:—
why, one might as well expect them to believe
that they themselves are but bubbles dancing
on the foaming stream of Time, or shadows
flickering across the infinite void ; that all existence is a dream, and everything is nothing !

But such intense religious emotions, such
vivid realizations of spiritual things as these to
which we are appealing, are they indeed well
enough established facts of human experience to
warrant our inference from them of a real and
distinct spiritual element in human nature?
Exceptional phenomena fail to afford a sufficiently secure basis of induction. They may
possibly be misinterpreted, and the generaliza-
tion from them run in an erroneous direction.
We need a wide array of facts to allow us to
feel safe in our inference.

Here, then, we are thrown back on the historical development of the religious instinct, and to
make our conclusions sure we must feel our way
along this line of human growth.

That religion is indigenous to human nature,
and springs up in it by a natural growth as a
legitimate and normal product of its unfolding
faculties and properties, may fairly be taken
as certain. If religion have not this native

character, but be something artificial and alien, it would be difficult to alight upon any one property or affection exhibited by men against which the same charge might not be brought. Possibly there may have existed, or even still be discoverable, a few rude and barbarous tribes among which no religious ideas can be distinctly traced; but as far as experience goes, the invariable concomitant of the absence of religion is found to be extreme backwardness in the development of all the higher and more characteristic qualities of humanity. No nation has ever existed in historic times without a religion; and not even the most barbarous tribes have failed to entertain a religion, as soon as their minds began to expand with culture, and human thoughts to predominate over merely animal instincts. Hence religion may be confidently said to be native to human nature, and to exist even in the lowest and rudest specimens of mankind as a germ, which only needs opportunity to grow and manifest itself.

Next, it may be affirmed that the essence of religion is the sense of relation to a superhuman Personality. How can it be otherwise? Religion implies worship, trust, reverence, prayer; these must have an object, and that object must

be of the nature of a Person. At times indeed
men have conceived themselves to be subject to
some impersonal Fate, Destiny, or Force ; but
that has never been the object towards which
their religious emotions have gone out. The
Beings whom they have worshipped have been
Beings from whom they hoped to obtain help
in their struggle against the blind, impersonal
Power ; personal Beings whose wills might be
moved by sacrifice, prayer, or worship. Unless
there is a Person to be worshipped, as well as a
person to offer the worship, religion is a name
without substance or signification.

Further, it is historically true of all religions
which have laid hold of the human heart, and
been efficacious to restrain and guide it, that
their strength has been in proportion to the
vividness with which they led men to realize
their relation to a superhuman Personality. So
far as religions were the mere creations of
poetical fancy or philosophic thought, they were
inefficient and barren ; it was the element in
them whereby they spoke to the universal
conscience, and awoke in it the sense of being
face to face with the awful, unseen Personality,
which swayed the hearts of men, and was fruitful of moral results.

We may pause here to remark that the old

atheistical account of the genesis of religion,
" It was fear which invented the gods," expresses but a half-truth. Man, in the presence
of the forces of Nature and the ills of life, may
have been oppressed by fear; but why did his
fear impel his mind in this particular direction,
and make him people heaven with deities? The
irrational brute cowers in terror before the
storm, but no one imagines it to go on to conceive of a supernatural being of whose wrath the
storm is an expression. How then came primitive man to make, as it is alleged, this step in
advance, and from the emotion of fear to rise to
the belief in a god to be feared? The only
intelligible explanation is, because he was not
an irrational brute, but a human being in whose
nature the germ of religion, the sense of relation
to an invisible Personality, already existed,
although as yet undeveloped and inoperative.
So that the account of the matter would have to
be amended, by presupposing that there was
already latent in man a god-inventing faculty, a
native tendency to conceive of a deity in relation to himself; and then adding, that under
the stimulus of fear this indigenous faculty was
first evoked into action, and produced the
consciousness of superior beings entitled to his
worship. Without this native instinct of re-

ligion, the growth of a theology out of fear
would be inexplicable.

Our glance back has shown us that when
religions have been practical forces in the world,
more or less vivid emotions towards the Object
of worship have been their legitimate effect, and
the measure of their vital affinity to human
nature. But we still want more definite
examples of the development of a consciousness
of God, to illustrate the working of the
spiritual faculty under favourable conditions.
For these examples we may go at once to the
two great and closely connected religions,
Judaism and Christianity, which in force and
fruitfulness have immeasurably surpassed all
others.

It is true that none of the great Gentile
religions which have really swayed the souls of
men has been entirely destitute of witness to the
spirituality of human nature. In the records
of them all may be traced aspirations towards
the Absolute and Infinite, yearnings for God, a
consciousness of vital relation to Him, a sense
of His being man's centre of repose and source
of blessedness. But in comparison with the
testimony borne by the sacred literature both
of Israel and Christendom, and by the history of the Christian church, all other wit-

ness is meagre and scarcely noticeable. It is
in this line of religious growth alone that the
spiritual instinct has had free development,
and risen into commanding and unrivalled
supremacy.

We open the Hebrew Scriptures, and from
beginning to end we find them pervaded by an
intense consciousness of God.   The writers are
numerous, of different ranks and classes, and
ranging over many hundreds of years; but
they have this common characteristic, that to
all of them God is manifestly the most real of
all beings, all existences, within their experience.   In comparison with Him they deem
everything else unsubstantial.   He is God, and
there is none else.   Earth and sky, and the
generations of mankind, are fleeting and shadowy
beside Him, who is always the same, the one
great Reality, the Eternal, the Infinite, the
Supreme. It is, moreover, distinctly as a Person
that they are conscious of Him, a Person who
thinks and wills, rules and loves and hates,
shows mercy and executes righteous judgment.
Whether it be a subject for praise or blame,
this anthropomorphism, this attributing to the
eternal God all the characteristics of personality
as we conceive of them in our own consciousness, is common to all the writers; a God who

is an impersonal law or tendency or power is
absolutely unknown to them.

Accordingly God is not only the centre of their
thoughts, but fills their hearts, and is the
supreme object of their affections. No words
can more passionately express longing, reverence,
trust, hope, gratitude, than those which they
continually pour out to this unseen Being.
Before Him they abase themselves in dust and
ashes. For Him their souls cry out with
fervent desire. In Him they are confident,
though all men rise up against them. He is
their refuge and fortress, their light and salva-
tion, the strength of their hearts and their
portion for ever. The words of His lips are
more precious to them than thousands of gold
and silver. He is the tender Father who knows
whereof they are made; the gracious Friend who
teaches and consoles them; the condescending
Monarch who lifts up the humble to dwell with
Him ; the All-perfect and holy and good, to
whom their souls are ever gravitating with
irrepressible admiration, thankfulness, and love,
crying out, " Bless the Lord, O my soul, and
all that is within me, bless His holy name."

In all this outpouring of religious emotion
what we are to observe is the intense consciousness of God which it exhibits, the vivid sense

of His reality, His goodness, His intimate relation to men. When we are told by philosophical analysts of human nature that any real
knowledge of God is impossible to it, and that
the God of human belief is nothing but an
ideal conception, an abstract thought, a shadow
formed by the imagination and destitute of
objective reality; we have, if we accept the
statement, to account for the remarkable fact
that to a most energetic race, which played a
prominent part in the development of mankind,
a merely ideal or fantastic conception was the
grandest and most absolute of realities, a bare
abstract thought a Presence nearer to them and
more vividly felt than anything in the world
of sense, a Presence which haunted them by
day and by night, searched their most secret
thoughts, filled them with reverential awe,
restrained them from evil ways, and guided
their souls in the paths of virtue. For instance,
we must imagine men of practical sense and
energy addressing a fiction of the imagination
in the following strain :—

"O Lord, Thou hast searched me and known
me. Thou knowest my downsitting and mine
uprising, Thou understandest my thought afar
off. Thou compassest my path and my lying
down, and art acquainted with all my ways.

For there is not a word in my tongue, but lo,
O Lord, Thou knowest it altogether.   Thou
hast beset me behind and before, and laid
Thine hand upon me. . . . . Whither shall I
go from Thy spirit? or whither shall I flee
from Thy presence?   If I ascend up into
heaven, Thou art there; if I make my bed in
hell, behold Thou art there.   If I take the wings
of the morning, and dwell in the uttermost
parts of the sea; even there shall Thy hand
lead me, and Thy right hand shall hold me.   If
I say, Surely the darkness shall cover me, even
the night shall be light about me.   Yea, the
darkness hideth not from Thee, but the night
shineth as the day; the darkness and the light
are both alike to Thee. . . . . Search me, O God,
and know my heart; try me, and know my
thoughts; and see if there be any way of
wickedness in me, and lead me in the way everlasting " (Psalm cxxxix).

Listening to such strains as this, we cannot
doubt that a personal living God, holy and
merciful, was the central conception of Judaism,
gathering round it the supreme reverence,
adoration, and trust of the nation of Israel.
From Judaism the same conception passed on
into Christianity, which indeed developed it
even more fully, and made it in its highest

imaginable perfection the common heritage of all Christian nations.

Christianity is built upon the Person of Jesus Christ, and holds forth His human character as the one flawless realization of humanity, the perfect exemplar, the absolute pattern, the unapproachable goal towards which all human aspiration and effort are to be unceasingly directed. Now of that character, as depicted in the Gospels, the moving force and energy was His intense consciousness of God as His Father. His Father's will was His sole rule of action; His Father's work the entire business of His life. In communion with His Father lay the secret of His strength; in conscious oneness with His Father the sum of His sinless perfection. He did not speak His own, but His Father's word; He did not seek His own, but His Father's glory; He did not act in His own name, or by His own authority, but by power and commission from His Father. Thus His life was consciously based on God, and led in God; in an uninter-rupted sense of the divine presence; in direct and constant intercourse of His soul with God; in the perpetual reception of truth and wisdom and strength from God. So close, so intimate, so perfect and absolute, was the relation between

Him and His Father, as to transcend description except by words which seem to imply that His own personality was almost absorbed and lost in His Father's; " I and My Father are one."

Such is the Christ of the Gospels. For our present purpose it does not matter whether His matchless character is considered as historical, or merely ideal. For even if ideal, it is the ideal which has been accepted by Christendom, that is by all the most energetic and enlightened nations of the world, as exhibiting the perfect pattern to which every human being should aim at being conformed. The Christian idea, therefore, of man—that is, let us remember, the idea of man which has rooted itself universally among all the leading, imperial races of man-kind—is not the agnostic idea of a being limited to the relations and experiences of this visible world; but of a being in direct and supreme relation to a heavenly Father, and living his entire life in the consciousness of that relation. A man without the conscious-ness of God is, in the estimate of the universal mind of Christendom, as distant and alien from the true ideal of humanity, as a man destitute of reason and moved only by the instincts of the animal life.

In strict accordance with the character of

Christ is the doctrine taught by Christianity, and accepted by all Christian nations as the highest attainable truth. So far from representing God as unknowable or distant, or hardly to be apprehended by human thought, it announces itself as the revelation of God's Fatherhood, proclaims Christ as "the way" by whom all men may come to the Father, teaches faith in God as the moving force of the only life worthy of man, sums up human excellence in love to God and through God to man, and holds forth the direct spiritual intuition of God as the transcendent recompense of striving after goodness. "Blessed," it says, "are the pure in heart, for they shall SEE GOD."

Such is Christianity, the religion above all others of the closest, most intensely realized, relation to the invisible God. But, it may be asked, has this religion which aims so high been able to root itself practically and effectually in human nature? Or has its doctrine of conscious, intimate, loving fellowship with the eternal, unseen God stood before the world as a splendid speculation only, a soaring aspiration of the idealizing faculty, a romance of the religious instinct, beautiful, magnificent, but inoperative and barren?

Let Christendom answer. Let its apostles,

its martyrs, its confessors, its philanthropists, its pure and saintly souls, answer. The millions upon millions who have learnt to cry, " Abba, Father ;" who have lived by their faith in God, and endured " as seeing Him who is invisible ;" whose hearts have been on fire with the love of God; who living have offered themselves daily sacrifices to Him, and dying have commended themselves into His hands; let them answer. Without faltering or hesitation, from the learned and the illiterate, from philosopher and artisan, from noble and peasant, from old and young, from the renowned and the lowly, from every breast in which for more than eighteen centuries the spirit of Christ has found a welcome and a home, comes back with one consentient voice the reply, " Truly our fellowship is with the Father, and with His Son Jesus Christ. We know that the Son of God is come, and hath given us an understanding that we may know Him that is true ; and we are in Him that is true, even in His Son Jesus Christ. This is the true God, and eternal life " (1 John i. 3 ; v. 20).

In the face of this mighty development of the religious instinct or sentiment among the choice and foremost races of mankind,—a development which may truly be said to have been an efficient cause rather than a mere accompaniment of their civilization,—it seems impossible with any show of reason to deny to human nature an indigenous faculty for religion, a faculty which reaches out instinctively beyond time and sense to find the eternal and infinite, and fastens itself on the idea of a fatherly God as the goal of its aspirations and the satisfaction of its desires. Who that fairly ponders on the prevalence and practical working of Judaism and Christianity can seriously account for the phenomena on any other hypothesis than the existence in man of this spiritual sense, tendency, or consciousness, as an essential, native element of his humanity ? To say that there have been tribes of men who exhibited no signs of possessing it, or even that there may possibly have been an early stage in the evolution of the human race in which the faculty had not yet come into being, does not really touch the root of the question at all. The most thorough-going evolutionist, who is driven by the exigencies of his theory to entertain the notion, in the teeth of all moral evidence, of the slow growth of the beast into the human being, must, if he still allows himself to think, be aware of the absurdity of denying a faculty to the mature man, because it had not appeared when he was

M

still half beast and but half man. What we know is this, that wherever human nature is not manifestly maimed, incomplete, crushed under barbarism and ignorance, that is, wherever it is human nature, there this spiritual faculty in fuller or scantier degree manifests itself in yearnings after the unseen, in the consciousness of relation to a superhuman Personality, in religious emotions, in acts of worship and thanksgiving. And we know too that in proportion as human nature has unfolded its higher properties, and advanced in the direction of its ideal type, in the same degree has the spiritual faculty invariably come out in greater force, and played a more dominant part in human life. These are the facts with which our induction must deal ; and from these we cannot but draw the conclusion, that just as certainly as man has a reasoning faculty, an æsthetic faculty, and a moral faculty, so surely does he also possess a spiritual faculty, by which he forms conceptions of God, yearns to know God, becomes conscious of God, and seeks repose in God's fatherly goodness and love.

Now it is true that this is purely a subjective conclusion, and that no logic can possibly carry us on from it to the objective fact of a real God who corresponds to the spiritual faculty in man.

But it is no such logical bridge from the subjective to the objective that our argument requires.
Again and again we have insisted that the whole
of the practical knowledge on which human life
is based rests on no logical foundation, but on
the trustworthiness of our instinctive consciousness and intuitive perceptions. We do trust
these, and it is only through trusting them
that we are enabled to live human lives. We
have no other ground for our belief in the physical world, in our fellow-men, or even in our
own permanent personality. Domestic, social,
national life, the administration of justice, the
acquisition of knowledge, the pursuit of Art,
the entire fabric of civilization, rest on these
primary instinctive perceptions, and the beliefs
of reason in which they embody themselves.
Why then should we begin to distrust our consciousness, and cast doubts on its veracity, as
soon as it begins to witness to us of God? If
our souls are conscious of Him, why should we
not believe that He really exists, just as much
as we believe that other minds and other objects
exist solely because we are conscious of them?
If we begin to doubt here, where shall our
doubting end? Experience proves that there
is a vision of God by the purified soul, just as
truly as there is a vision of the beauteous face

of Nature by the sensitive eye; why stigmatize
the one as a dream of the imagination, while we
confess the other to be a reality of practical experience and common sense?

This part of our argument may now be briefly
summed up in a few words.

By tracing the history and working of the
religious instinct we reach the broad fact, that
a consciousness of God is one of the primary
and fundamental intuitions of human nature.
Whence the conclusion follows, that the belief in
God to which it has given rise among mankind
is one of those primary beliefs of the reason
which underlie all logical proof, and justify
themselves by their existence.

CHAPTER VIII.

THE STRENGTH GIVEN TO THE PROOF OF THEISM BY THE CONVERGENCE OF THE SEVERAL ARGUMENTS.

HAVING now pursued our inquiry along several independent lines, and found ourselves led by each to the same conclusion, it remains for us briefly to notice how greatly the argument is strengthened by the convergence of its several branches, and what a high degree of moral probability is thereby imparted to the result. To this object the present short chapter will be devoted.

The force which is given to testimony by the coincidence and mutual support of independent witnesses is familiar to every one who has any practical acquaintance with the laws of evidence. A single witness may not improbably be mistaken or false, but that two independent witnesses should concur in the same error or falsehood is extremely unlikely; and with every

addition to the number of independent witnesses
the improbability of their all agreeing in the
same mistake or lie is enormously augmented,
and soon reaches what we call moral impossibility. The same principle holds good in all
investigations into the truth of things : the
most surely established theories or facts derive
their moral certainty from the coincidence, or
consilience, as it has been called, of diverse and
independent proofs.

But as our argument aims at being cast in a
popular and easy form, we are not content to
leave the matter in this abstract shape, and will
endeavour to frame an illustration to show how
the convergence of several testimonies to the
same conclusion practically compels the mind to
accept it.

Our imaginary case is as follows :—A hundred years ago first appeared a book which has
since become celebrated, but the authorship of
which has been veiled in such secrecy that
nothing is certain about it, beyond the fact that
the conjectures of the curious have often pointed
to a particular person as not unlikely to have
written it. The book, we suppose, has marked
features. It deals with contemporary individuals and transactions in a strain indicating
familiar acquaintance and strong personal in-

terest, praising and censuring with a free hand,
and frequently on grounds which seem to indicate the writer's partialities and antipathies
rather than a dispassionate exercise of judgment.
The style is elaborate and artificial, abounding
in carefully-wrought points, illustrations, and
sarcasms; and many allusions betray a technical knowledge of a special branch of science
remote from the ordinary studies of politi-
cians.

At length a discovery is made which throws
a flood of light on the mystery. The ancient
home of the person to whom conjecture has
generally pointed as the possible author passes
into the hands of an owner, who is resolved to
explore every nook and corner for traces of a
connexion between its former occupant and the
celebrated work; and the result is the finding,
carefully concealed in a wall, of a box containing
the following documents, all in a handwriting
which is identified with that of undoubted
letters and signatures of the individual in
question.

1. A manuscript of the entire work, not in
fair copy for the printer, but scored with the
erasures, interlineations, and corrections, which
show the author at work in the act of composing.

2. A diary, recording day by day the writer's share in public transactions and feelings about his contemporaries, such as to account for the knowledge and sentiments expressed in the published work.

3. A set of note-books containing a number of the extracts from other authors quoted in the published book, and rough drafts of many of the more elaborate illustrations, similes, and satirical allusions.

4. A bundle of notes of lectures and class-room work, showing that the writer had for some time studied, at an early period of his life, the particular branch of science with which the book betrays a special acquaintance.

Here are clearly four separate and independent links of connexion between the book and the conjectured author. The first shows him composing it; the second, leading the life which corresponded to it; the third, collecting the materials for some of its most characteristic portions; the fourth, acquiring the special knowledge which is almost unconsciously betrayed in it. The discovery of any one of these links would have been sufficient to settle the question of the authorship in the mind of any competent judge of literary evidence, but the combination of the four is so irresistible that not the most scrupulous jury in the world would hesitate to convict a man capitally on evidence of equal strength.

Yet we can conceive of an obstinate sceptic making a show of holding out against even this accumulation and coincidence of proofs. "You are resting on inferences," he might say, "each of which is insecure, because it is drawn from a fact of which some other explanation than yours is possible. All that has been discovered may be the product of an elaborate forgery on the part of your supposed author, who may have laid this gigantic train of fraud to impose a falsehood on the world in after-times. To convince me I ought to have seen him with my own eyes actually at work, thinking out the pages as his hand wrote them; or in default of ocular witness I want the direct testimony of spectators who saw him at work, of friends who listened to his avowal of the book, of the printer who received the manuscript from him, of his own conduct in bearing sundry unpleasant consequences of the book without complaint or protest."

So the obstinate sceptic might argue; but we may be sure that the common sense of the world would no more heed his objections, than the ocean heeds the scream of the wild fowl which wander over its heaving breast.

Now, from our parable let us return to the
great question which we have in hand.

The work of which we have sought to discover the Author is the whole universe of being,
known to us by experience, comprising ourselves, our fellow-men, and the vast physical
cosmos. There is a reputed Author of it, from
whom in the common belief of mankind it
originated, a personal, righteous, fatherly God;
and our task has been to discover, if possible,
trustworthy evidence which may enable the
inquiring mind to repose with satisfaction in this
belief.

The result of our investigation has been the
discovery of four different lines of evidence, each
of which conducts us to God.

1. Viewing the universe in the light of our
own consciousness of originating will, the existence of a supreme Will is borne in on our minds
as the only conceivable Cause of its existence.

2. Viewing Nature in the light of our own
consciousness of designing intelligence, the existence of a supreme Intelligence is borne in on
our minds as the only conceivable Source of its
order, its organisms, and its relations.

3. Viewing our own moral faculty as revealed
to us in our consciousness, and through observation of its various manifestations, the existence of

a supreme righteous Lawgiver to whom we are accountable is borne in on our minds, as the only sufficient explanation of the voice of conscience, the sense of responsibility, and the working force of the moral sentiment.

4. Viewing our own spiritual faculty, as revealed to us in our consciousness, through the aspirations which reach out towards the infinite, the affections which yearn for a supreme Object, and the intuitions which realize the presence of the infinite and adorable Goodness, the existence of a heavenly Father is borne in on our minds, as the only satisfactory means of accounting for the phenomena of the spiritual life of mankind.

Here are four separate lines of evidence, originating in as many distinct branches of our consciousness, and leading through the observation of different classes of phenomena to the same great conclusion, namely GOD.

For will, intelligence, morality, spirituality, taking them in the senses in which they have been defined, are attributes essentially different from each other, each giving rise to its own series of the effects by which our personality exhibits its properties. If then each by itself is a witness, more or less definite and forcible, by which the existence of God is attested, their agreement in leading to a common conclusion is the convergence of four independent witnesses, and the result has the moral force which we have seen to arise from such a coincidence of testimony.

But the sceptic is not satisfied. He asks for some more direct, more palpable proof. "These proofs which you offer," he says somewhat scornfully, " are only statements of the way in which your own consciousness unfolds itself. They prove nothing but its subjective properties. You cannot expect me to accept God as an actual reality, merely because you find Him in your own thought. It is a Being, not an idea, of which I am in search. If God really exists, show Him to me, either to my reason or my perception, and I will bow down and worship."

Here is the unreasonableness of agnosticism. Evidence which in every other province of life is considered sufficient is in this debate about the basis of religion set aside as of no cogency, and a demand is made for proof of a kind which in the nature of things is unattainable.

" Demonstrate God to my reason," says the agnostic. Well, we must have some axioms or postulates to start with, or demonstration is impracticable. But what shall they be ? *Everything must have had a cause.* " Stop ! " cries our friend, "that is exactly what I do not know; for anything that I can see, matter and force may have been eternal." We try again: *Order universally implies mind.* "That is much more than I can admit," is the rejoinder; "order may very likely be the result of some unintelligent principle of production." We make another attempt: *Design implies a designer.* "Worse still," is the reply; "the phrase is either an identical proposition, like *A work of art implies an artist,* and in that case virtually begs the question; or else it is an assertion incapable of proof, inasmuch as no one can be sure that organisms have not grown into being under the impulse of a natural evolutionary force, without any conscious designer of their structure." It is plain by this time that there are no axioms or postulates on which we can agree to base the argument, and hence the demand for a demonstration of God to the reason is in its nature unreasonable.

But the agnostic gives us an alternative. "If you cannot prove God to my reason by convincing argument, at least make Him in some way manifest to my perceptions."

It is an old complaint, "Except ye see signs and wonders, ye will not believe." In what conceivable way can mind or spirit be manifested to the human organs of perception? They can take cognizauce of phenomena only, and God is not a phenomenon. If we could have looked on while He was in the very act of creating, all we should have seen would have been the creatures as they started into physical existence; the omnipotent Agent would have been invisible. If we could hear the voice of God out of the sky, all we should be sensible of would be a sound, and of that we should still have to ascertain the cause. Or suppose the demand for sensible proof took the form of a challenge of the most High : "If Thou art, veil the meridian sun in darkness." Who could expect the Eternal to deign a reply? And even if He condescended to answer, and the radiant orb suddenly faded into gloom, sensible proof of God there would be none. Still would it be open to the daring challenger to discuss the origin of the strange phenomenon, and to ascribe it to accidental coincidence, physical causes, or the agency of beings other than a supreme Author of all things. Sensible proof of God is in the nature of things impossible, and therefore the demand for it must be pronounced unreasonable.

Putting aside then the claim of the determined sceptic for either logical demonstration or

perceptible manifestation of God as inapplicable
and unmeaning, it only remains to fall back on
the indirect evidence for God which comes
through our consciousness.   To enable us fairly
to estimate the force of this, two considerations
must be borne in mind.

First, that it really is on evidence of this kind
that the whole of our practical knowledge is
based.   There is not a single object outside a
man's personality, of the existence of which he
is certified either by logical proof or direct
perception.   Of his own sensations, feelings,
emotions he has direct knowledge, but of nothing
else whatever.   It is from these that he leaps
by an instinctive inference to the belief of a
world outside him, of fellow-men like himself,
and even of the identity and permanence of his
own individual self.   By an instinctive inference,
we repeat, not by a process of logic ; that certain
fact is the key of our whole position.   These
primary beliefs are utterly incapable of demonstration ; they spring up of themselves in the
mind ; they are intuitive, indigenous, the offspring of a rational instinct, but no logical
justification of them is possible.   Yet they are
practically. irresistible, and no sane person
refuses to act upon them.   If a metaphysician
questions them speculatively in his closet, he

does not the less make them the basis of his life, as soon as he steps out to converse with his family or mix with the world. Illogical they are, but inevitable, and ineradicably rooted in human nature. If then it can be shown that belief in God springs up in a similar way, and rests substantially on the same foundation of instinctive inference, it will need no further justification, and the charge brought against it of lacking logical demonstration will be irrelevant.

And secondly, we have before us ample evidence that belief in God actually has that relation to the human mind which we call instinctive or intuitive, in that it springs up or roots itself universally in the consciousness, and takes ever firmer hold in proportion to the growth of man in the higher characteristics of humanity. Moreover, we find that, in seeking for a rational ground for the belief, it is not along one line only, but along four distinct and independent lines that our minds advance to the assured possession of it. From our own consciousness of will we infer a supreme, originating Will; of intelligence, a supreme, constructing Mind; of morality, a supreme righteous Lawgiver; of spirituality, a supreme Father. Thus the instinctive inference of a personal God is woven of four separate strands; the evidence is the

coincident testimony of four independent witnesses; the proof is the combination and
consilience of four distinct lines of induction.
And our conclusion is, that belief in God rests
on as trustworthy and practically sure a foundation as any of those primary instinctive beliefs
of the reason on which all mankind habitually
rely and act.

CHAPTER IX.

THE PRACTICAL VINDICATION OF THEISM BY ITS WORKING IN THE WORLD.

WE remarked some way back that a belief which is of a practical nature may be in some degree tested by its working. After we have examined its foundations, and found it to strike its roots in the general affections and constitutional structure of the human mind, we may go on to watch it in action, and observe whether the influence exerted by it over the life and growth of mankind is of such a nature as to evince its vital power for good, and thus to furnish an experimental justification of its existence.

The great instinctive beliefs to which reference has so often been made, our beliefs in the Self within each of us, the Selves of our fellow-men, and the external universe, certainly work with admirable effect, and are the basis of all human life, society, and progress. Without them knowledge and civilization would be impossible, and mankind would be no better than a bestial herd. They are thus approved and verified by their effects. To doubt of them may perhaps be possible for the recluse in his cell, but to maintain the doubt in the midst of the busy world is the exclusive achievement of the insane.

But is a practical verification of belief in God by observation of its working in any degree possible? Can we trace its effects along the line of human development, so as to arrive at the conclusion that it has been sufficiently fruitful of good to approve itself as a legitimate and ennobling possession of the human mind? If this can be satisfactorily done, we shall undoubtedly feel the hold of the belief upon our reason strengthened, and the induction by which we justified it appreciably confirmed.

Now to ascertain with precision the consequences arising from belief in God, we should need to institute a careful comparison on a wide scale between the history of races of men who entertained that belief, and the history of other races of men among whom it had no footing. But this is in fact impracticable, because we are not acquainted with any race of mankind which has been nurtured in atheism. The belief in God, whether it be innate, or instinctive, or traditionary, or suggested by experience, has

N 2

possessed such an attraction or affinity for the human mind that in some form or other it has rooted itself everywhere, and exerted a dominant influence over the growth of all known civilizations, both ancient and modern. Mingled, indeed, it has often been with much superstition, and held in very imperfect forms, especially in the earlier stages of human development, and among races which have been remarkable for their backwardness in unfolding the higher elements of humanity.	Still, wherever men have formed human societies and grown into nations, there the belief in some shape has existed, moulding and tempering their minds and habits, and exercising a formative power over their institutions, their laws, and their morality.	A really atheistic community would be a phenomenon of which the world has hitherto had no experience.

Two exceptions to this statement may perhaps be alleged, which it is only fair to notice.

The first need not detain us more than a moment. It is said that travellers have occasionally discovered small tribes of men among whom no traces of theistic belief could be detected. Such tribes have invariably been in the lowest stage of debasement and ignorance; without writing or art, or anything that savours of civilization;

scarcely intelligible in their speech, unsociable, inhospitable, and retiring from strangers within the fence of a sullen reserve. To arrive at any certainty about the religious belief of such tribes could in few cases be an easy matter, and subsequent visitors have not seldom found reason to correct the impressions reported by those who first made acquaintance with them. But whatever may have been the precise condition of these few exceptional tribes, it can no more tell against the universality of the instinct which leads to belief in God, than the absence of intelligence in infants and idiots can tell against the universality of the endowment of mankind with the faculty of reason. So far as any inference can be drawn from them it would be that atheism is associated with only the lowest and most debased stage of human nature; an inference which can scarcely be of much value to the opponents of theism.

The other apparent exception is more considerable. It is created by the wide prevalence of Buddhism, which is reckoned to be the religion at the present time of nearly one-third part of mankind. This system is described as an organized and systematic atheism. It teaches no belief in God; and four hundred millions of the human race in Eastern Asia are said to live

and die in it, contented and wishing for nothing
better.

This is a portentous fact, and one which at
first sight seems to invalidate the claim of theism
to be considered as having in any real sense an
instinctive basis in human nature. But a little
examination will show that the fact is far from
having so wide and decisive a signification.

We know from historic records that Buddhism
was by no means a primitive or slowly evolved
religion, but arose at a definite period as a reaction against a very complex polytheistic religion,
burdened with an oppressive doctrine of endless
transmigrations, and a tyrannical system of caste.
It sprang full-grown from the mind of a man
of melancholy genius, a pure-hearted, amiable
dreamer, who brooded over the miseries of his
countrymen till a way of deliverance seemed to
shape itself in his labouring thought. It was a
way which none but an Oriental mystic could
have conceived. All human misery, he taught,
arises from human desire. Let men renounce
their individuality, extinguish their desires, and
reduce themselves to impersonal shadows, here
to-day and gone to-morrow, and misery will
cease. Life is but an uneasy dream, from which
the blessed awaking is the extinction of all sensation and all consciousness. In that tranquil

haven of passionless insensibility and nothingness suffering men may find a final refuge from
their sorrows, if only they will live together in
peace, banish every desire from their hearts, and
labour to attain a state of perfect indifference
and quiescence.

Such was the doctrine of the founder or
Buddhism. Two very different elements were
obviously combined in it; a strange, incoherent
metaphysic, and the germ of a social reforma-
tion. The former denied human personality,
and resolved men into casual bundles of organs,
destitute of any permanent Self. The latter
abolished the tyranny of caste, introduced the
ideas of fraternity and equality, and by stig-
matizing desire as the one prolific evil to be
fought against and vanquished, laid the axe to
the root of the strifes and crimes and vices by
which so large a share of human misery has
ever been caused.

Now if we look at this strange system in the
light of its practical operation, several things of
great importance to our estimate of it will soon
become apparent.

First, even in theory it was not so much
atheism as what has been called NIHILISM, the
negation of everything but transient phenomena.
It did not so much deny God as pass Him by as

irrelevant and needless. What it denied was
humanity. Reducing man to an impersonal
shadow, disquieted by the existence of desire,
and to be laid to unconscious rest by the extinction of desire, it had no point at which a doctrine about God could come into relation to it.
It had therefore nothing to say about God, and
in this sense was atheistic.

Next, the power and charm of the system lay
in its social element, far more than in its metaphysical basis. Nature was too strong to allow
the latter to enter with any real force into men's
hearts. The masses could not be persuaded out
of their personality, could not even. comprehend
the demand to regard themselves as impersonal
shadows. All the incoherent mysticism fell
unheeded on their ears. But the system eman-
cipated them from the intolerable tyrannies of
caste, and promoted peaceful fellowship and
tranquil existence ; and to those oppressed and
rest-loving populations of the East this was as
attractive as sleep to the pain-stricken and
weary.

Further, Buddhism in practice is very far
indeed from being atheistic. It could not
live without a god and a worship, and by the
instinct of its adherents it was soon transformed
into a practically theistic system. The lands

where it finds a home are covered with temples, which have their priests, their ceremonies, and their offerings. Buddha himself has become a deity to his disciples, and the state of extinction or unconsciousness to which his doctrine points has assumed to the popular mind the aspect of a delicious paradise of repose. Moreover, alongside of the worship of Buddha there has, at least in some quarters, grown up a supplementary worship of deities of a subordinate kind, by which the system has become a sort of incongruous polytheism. So that, on the whole, Buddhism, in its historical aspect, bears witness rather for than against the hypothesis of an instinctive tendency in human nature to believe in God.

Once more, whatever Buddhism is theoretically, in its actual working it is the religion of stagnation. Among none but dreamy, listless, unprogressive Orientals could it have survived a single generation. Not one iota has it ever contributed to the development of mankind; not a single leader of our race has ever sprung from its bosom. It is the religion of a starved, stunted, torpid humanity, possible only when man is little more than half human, and utterly incompatible with the life, the energy, and the intellectual culture of the Western world.

Thus this great apparent exception to the universality of theistic belief fades away on examination, and leaves our position intact, that no race of mankind known to history has ever really been nurtured in atheism.

But if it is impracticable to compare the results of theism and atheism in their influence on the development of races, because no instance of atheistic development can be found, might we not institute a comparison between man and man, and ascertain whether the individual atheist suffers by being placed alongside of his theistic brethren ?

Here again a difficulty will be found, sufficiently great to invalidate any results favourable to atheism to which such a comparison might possibly lead us. The disturbing effects of heredity, education, and environment cannot be accurately estimated. The individual atheist comes of a line of theistic ancestors, from whom he inherits moral and intellectual habitudes and tendencies which underlie his personal unbelief, and largely modify its effects unknown to, and perhaps in spite of, himself. His own education has probably been a theistic one, and the entire social atmosphere in which he lives is certainly impregnated with theism. Suppose him, then, to be irreproachable in morals, upright, temperate, kindly, a good citizen and an energetic worker for the benefit of his race; it would not be possible to determine how much of this excellence is due to the impressions stamped on his nature by his antecedents and environment, and how much is the genuine fruit of his personal atheistic sentiments. Hence a conclusion in favour of atheism, based on the fact that a few atheists of high moral qualities here and there exist, would certainly be untenable. But it is no less certain that if atheism were generally found to be associated with a low type of moral character, the fact would tell strongly against it. So that the result of a comparison between individuals, though it could not support the cause of atheism, might possibly do it serious damage.

It appears, then, that we shall be obliged to take a more circuitous route, to trace the practical working of theistic belief in the world. To do it fairly, as becomes sincere seekers after truth, we must bear in mind the conditions under which belief in God has had to work.

Let us bring before our minds a race of men in a primitive stage, ignorant, superstitious, animated by strong animal instincts and fierce passions; and let us imagine a belief in an unseen, superhuman Ruler to spring up among them. Could we expect it to assume at once in

their minds the character of a pure and refined
monotheism, such as a Christian philosopher
holds, and to transform them at a stroke into a
virtuous and peaceable community? Surely the
expectation would be absurd! Ignorance and
superstition would be certain to clothe the belief
at first in grotesque forms, and to invest the invisible Power with passions too much resembling
those of mankind; and although the influence of
the belief, even when thus deteriorated, might be
on the whole for good, an appreciable progress in
virtue would probably be but slowly won against
the intractable passions and propensities of
human nature. Under such circumstances to
argue that the belief was good for nothing, because for a long time the result was so mixed
and imperfect, would be manifestly unfair and
irrational.

But suppose, as ages rolled by, that the race
gradually advanced to a higher level of civilization, and unfolded a fuller, riper humanity; that
the standard of morals rose, national and domestic virtues became common, passion was brought
under the restraints of principle, and unselfish
charity was enthroned at the summit of all
imaginable human perfection: and suppose further, that concurrently with this general culture
the theistic belief worked its way out of the low,

superstitious, or grotesque forms of its infancy, and grew into a pure spiritual monotheism, inextricably interwoven with the institutions, laws, morals, and hopes of the community, as the sustaining force of all that was best among them, and most conducive to human progress. In such a case would not an intelligent and impartial observer conclude that belief in God worked well, and threw its influence on the side of civilization and goodness? Could he help seeing in it a mighty factor of human development?

Now the history of the world does, in a general way, correspond with this imaginary sketch, and therefore we claim it as a witness to the practical working for good of the belief in God. That the belief has not yet triumphed over every evil passion, and converted the world into a paradise of peace and virtue, is, alas! but too true; but the fact is no proof that the belief is not steadily working on this line, and has not been a powerful agent in bringing mankind thus far on their way. Indeed, the only reasonable objection which we can anticipate to this account of the matter would be, that it was not so much the belief which promoted the growing civilization, as the impulse of civilization which carried on the belief, and put on it the polish of advancing knowledge and superior morality.

Well, suppose it were so; suppose that human nature does contain within itself a self-developing power by which it has grown out of barbarism, framed itself into well-ordered communities, and evolved out of its own thought a pure morality and a spiritual religion. In that case we should have this very remarkable and significant fact to explain; that the riper and more cultivated human nature grew, the more it became possessed and influenced by a pure and lofty theism. Had belief in God, however originally started, been a mere superstition, without foundation in reality, and incapable of promoting the progress of humanity, one would have expected it gradually to die out with the increase of knowledge, and the progress achieved by the real evolutionary forces of the intellectual and moral world. But if, on the contrary, it has not only held its own, but waxed in grandeur till it has filled the whole firmament of thought and emotion, and has gone on rooting itself deeper and deeper as human nature grew wiser and better, then we confidently ask, whether it can justly be considered as less than a belief which possesses an elemental affinity for human nature, and is the inseparable accompaniment of its true and complete culture.

But the allegation that belief in God has been only a consequence, and not at all a cause, of the progress of mankind in moral and spiritual culture, appears to us to derive no support from the general tenour of history. No doubt there is a sense in which civilization may be truly said to have reacted on the belief at various times, and helped to purify it from savage or superstitious incrustations. Gentler and more refined manners and feelings tend to soften even theological conceptions. Increase of secular knowledge rubs off crudities and excrescences from the popular ideas of the supernatural. A mutual action and reaction on each other of civilization and popular theism may fairly be affirmed. But to say that belief in a supreme Lord and Father has not been a mighty force in the world, and a force exerted in the main on the side of elevated and noble conduct, would be to contradict the most patent facts. All the higher heroisms by which the empire of self has been vanquished have been manifestly sustained by this belief; and it is by the attraction of these that mankind are stirred to a more generous and unselfish life. Ask the martyrs who bleed for their faith, the pioneers of the Gospel who pave the

way of the cross with their lives, the philanthropists who wear themselves out in labours of
charity, the pure souls whose resolve to preserve
an unstained conscience no temptation can
shake, the patient sufferers who are bright and
cheerful on their beds of pain; ask these the
secret of their strength, and with one voice
they will ascribe it to their consciousness of the
presence of God. Whence the authority with
which conscience speaks, the solemn sanction
which guards an oath, the secret dread which
mantles guilt with horror, the sting of intolerable remorse, and the irrepressible desire to make
reparation for wrong, but from the sense of a
supreme relation to an unseen God? Lower
motives and meaner forces may indeed have
done much to impel mankind along the path of
self-improvement; but that all the mightiest
spiritual forces which have wrought in the evolution of the noblest qualities of human nature
have sprung out of belief in God, the history of
all the foremost races of mankind unmistakeably
testifies.

But from these generalities let us pass on to
particular evidences of the beneficial energy
exerted by theism.

We have already remarked, that it is in the
phenomena of Judaism and Christianity that the

working of theism is most conspicuous. What then is the testimony borne by these?

Among all the remains of pre-Christian literature which have come down to our times, the Hebrew writings which are contained in the Old Testament stand out absolutely unrivalled and unique for their spiritual force. Grace, freshness, beauty, shine in the classic pages of Greece and Rome; and there we may discover treasures of poetry, art, and philosophy which the world will never be weary of admiring. But for lessons of righteousness, and for the culture of the spiritual life, we must go to the Hebrews. In this line their sacred literature stands alone. Art and philosophy are not to be learnt there; but it teaches us how to conquer self, rise above the senses, and live in the spirit. It is filled and saturated with the ideas of right and duty and moral obligation; its pages glow with a light and are instinct with a force which we feel to be not of the earth, but to come down as mighty and solemn influences from a higher sphere. This light and force have, accordingly, streamed from that literature ever since into the souls of men, quickening their spiritual consciousness, and never suffering them to fall back into the sensual life of paganism. Over the entire Western world it has exerted a regenerating

o

power, enthroning conscience above passion, right above might, duty above self-interest, and stamping on the human heart the ineffaceable conviction that a life of righteousness is the only life worthy of man.

The work begun by Hebraism was taken up and completed by Christianity. If the one impressed on the world the impulse of righteousness, the other set before it the portraiture of absolute goodness. In giving to mankind the matchless character of Jesus Christ, Christianity planted in the bosom of humanity the mightiest force that has ever worked for virtue, by the constraint of sweet persuasion and irresistible attractiveness. There all that Hebraism had taught by precept concerning a divine life was embodied in a living example; all that Hebraism had sketched in outline was filled up with lovely and perfect detail. There holiness was blended with tenderness, and duty was transfigured by love. From that character has flowed ceaselessly into Christendom a creative energy, from which have sprung the glory of meekness and patience, the grace of chivalrous self-devotion, the sweet affections and charities which cluster round wedded life, the peaceful home, and the blessed fellowship of faith and hope. Before the world that matchless character has ever since stood, as

the ideal of all possible human excellence, the
goal of the loftiest aspirations, the centre to
which the souls who· hunger and thirst after
righteousness have always gravitated with
adoring admiration, gratitude, and love.

Now that mighty impulse of righteousness
impressed on the world by Hebraism, and this
portraiture of perfect and most winning goodness set before the eyes of mankind by Christianity, were theistic to their very core. Out
of theism they sprang, of theism they were the
living, working embodiments. Every page of
that ancient literature burns with GOD. His
great name moves throughout it in solemn
majesty, as the one source of all its elevation
and power. To Him, Creator, Ruler, Father,
Judge, every eye is turned, every ear attentive,
every righteous heart faithful and true; His
power and glory, His holiness and goodness,
the wonders of His hands, the preciousness of
His word, these are the universal theme, which
kindles the imagination of the poet, points the
moral of the historian, and touches the lips of
the prophet with fire. There God is all in all.
And of the portraiture in the Christian Gospels
what can we say strong enough to convey its
full import ? To describe it as the creation of
theistic sentiment, or to show how every fea-

ture and line of it is instinct with belief in God,
and every grace and loveliness in it grows out
of the consciousness of God, would be to utter
but half the truth. It has been received and
adored by Christendom as theistic in a far
higher sense, even as the revelation under a
human form of God Himself. " He that hath
seen Me hath seen the Father," is the word
put into the mouth of the Christ; and Christendom gazing on Him has believed that it
gazed on " the image of the invisible God," and
beheld " the light of the knowledge of the glory
of God in the face of Jesus Christ."

Thus all that both Hebraism and Christianity
have done to elevate human life above the low,
sensuous level of paganism, must be credited to
theism, when we desire to make a fair estimate
of the way in which it has practically wrought
in the world. But though the conclusion might
then seem to be inevitable, that belief in God
has all that kind of verification which experience
of its effects can give to a practical belief, there
is still one way to be considered by which
escape has been sought from this conclusion.

" True," it has been said, " theism in some shape
was a necessary factor in human progress. Growing out of an instinct which personified natural
forces, it supplied the impulse required to tame

the wilder passions, and powerfully contributed to the development of mankind. But the time will come when it will have accomplished its work, and will disappear in the light of a riper knowledge of the universe. The evolution of humanity is ever bearing on the race to higher degrees of culture, and when the moral faculty has been thoroughly matured and attained un-disputed supremacy, man will be self-centred and become a perfect law to himself, and will no longer need the idea of God. Then the pro-visional beliefs of his childhood will be super-seded by scientific truth, and in the ripeness of intellectual and moral manhood he will at last become aware that there is nothing within the range of his vision diviner than himself."

Is it indeed so? we ask in amazement. Where are the signs of such a progress? Where a single token that the idea of God is being outgrown, and becoming needless to the world? Is it not still true that all the noblest develop-ments of human excellence cluster round the consciousness of God; all the fairest graces of purity, unselfishness, devotion to duty, self-sacrifice, and moral heroism, are the fruits of faith in God? Does not universal experience tell us that where belief in God has grown dim and faint, there retrogression has set in and

human nature has sunk to a lower level? Can
we forget the sentiment extorted from unbeliev-
ing lips in a wild outbreak of anarchical passions,
that even though there were no God it would
be necessary to invent one to keep society from
dissolution?

We have already seen, while investigating
the action of the moral sentiment, that no theory
of morals from which God is absent provides a
working force sufficient to sustain morality
against the onset of temptation and the violence
of human passion; and that reason is unable to
discover any adequate source of the power of
morality except faith in a living and righteous
God, who will insure the ultimate and everlasting coincidence of well-being with well-doing.
If this be true, it settles the question. A perfect human morality without God must then
be a dream which cannot be realized. Morality
might indeed for a season outlive theism. Inherited tendencies, the force of custom, the sur-
vival of modes of thinking, the memory of the satisfactions of virtue and the shame of guilt, might
continue to it a lingering existence, just as the
impulse of the fly-wheel keeps up the motion
of a machine for a time after the motive power
has been withdrawn. But so far as the result
can be foreseen by reason, an inevitable change

for the worse would soon manifest itself. Self-restraint would become weaker, selfishness gain the upper hand, the passions revolt more successfully; and at last before the din and anarchy of unbridled lawlessness the virtues would take their flight, finding room no more for their exercise in a world which had outgrown its belief in God.

CHAPTER X.

THE DIFFICULTIES OF THEISM NOT REALLY
SERIOUS.

OUR discussion will not be complete, without noticing the difficulties which may be said to beset the argument for theism, and are found by an increasing number of minds sufficiently formidable to make them hesitate to acknowledge its conclusiveness. These difficulties fall into two classes, the logical and the moral.

The first to be noticed is the one which has been familiar to us all through our inquiry; namely, the impossibility of rigorously proving the existence of God, either by demonstrative reasoning or strict induction from observed facts. Such a stupendous proposition as that which affirms the existence of a supreme Being, Lord and Judge of all, requires, it is said, a proportionately strong proof for its support. and the inferences from the subjective facts of the human consciousness are alleged to be unable to sustain its weight.

Our answer has been that if this be a fatal defect in the proof, it is a defect by no means peculiar to theism, but shared by it with every other branch of human belief and knowledge. Nothing whatever outside man's consciousness can be established by rigorous logical proof. All our beliefs run back into our consciousness for their ultimate ground, and finally rest on the veracity of our primary and instinctive convictions. Hence if this difficulty were allowed to be fatal, there would be no way of escape left from universal and absolute scepticism. And as we are not arguing with those who doubt everything, down even to their own identity, we hold that the answer is sufficient.

But it may be asked, " Why, then, do men of intelligence, who make no difficulty of admitting other beliefs which rest ultimately on the veracity of the human consciousness, raise a difficulty about this ground of belief when they come to theism? Students of the physical sciences, for instance, never for a moment doubt the objective reality of Nature, although the existence of that great object of their researches is only an instinctive inference from the sensations of which they are conscious. Must there not be some essential difference between the evidence on which Nature is accepted as real, and that which is produced on behalf of the objective reality of God ?"

There is a difference, certainly, but it is not a generic one, not one of nature and kind. The witness of the human consciousness is the common ground of both beliefs; of both it is true that they are instinctive beliefs of the reason, and are incapable of logical proof. But consciousness is not simple, but complex and many-sided. It has various departments, and some of these lie nearer, so to speak, to our daily life than others, and are more direct, obvious, and familiar. There are the consciousnesses of bodily sensation and appetite; of affection and passion; of artistic beauty; of necessary truth; of moral rectitude; of religious emotion. These are not all on a level, nor equally clear and forcible in all men; while some are universal and imperious, others require culture to bring them out, and reflection to interpret them, and may possibly, in some individuals, lie quiescent and unsuspected in some unawakened element of their nature.

Suppose, then, that to a man, in whom different kinds of consciousness were very unequally developed, two arguments were presented, one resting on facts of consciousness with which he was familiar, and the other on different facts of which he had little or no experience in consequence of his defect of culture on that side of his nature. It would be in the highest degree unlikely that the two arguments should be equally forcible and convincing to his mind. They might be alike valid and conclusive; but while in one he would find solid ground to go upon, the other could scarcely escape appearing unconvincing and shadowy.

This distinction is so important, that it is desirable by the use of illustrations to bring it to the test of experience. As our first illustration we will take the culture, in different directions, of the sense of hearing.

When we hear a sound, all we are conscious of is our own subjective sensation. Whether the sensation is produced by something outside us, of which we obtain information through our sense of hearing; or whether it is independent of any external object, like the imaginary sounds heard in dreams, or reverie, or states of nervous derangement; must in every case be a matter of inference, in making which our judgment is guided by previous culture and experience. Moreover, in the case of real sounds the faculty of perceiving, distinguishing, and comprehending them is largely due to the cultivation of the consciousness of sound.

Now let us take two persons in whom this consciousness has been developed in very diverse directions; let one be the highly-trained musician of the city, the other the wild hunter of the forests and prairies. Let them first go out together into the haunts of the roaming game; and as they creep stealthily along, every rustle and murmur and note will be caught and understood by the quick ear of the savage, while the musician will notice little and comprehend nothing. But let them then visit the concert-room of the city, while some grand chorus is rolled forth from a thousand instruments and throats, in swelling volumes of intricate and melodious harmony, and the parts of the listeners will be reversed. While every note speaks to the musician's soul, and the slightest deviation of tone is caught by his ear, the savage hears nothing but a roaring Babel of noise.

Why these immense differences of experience? Both are receiving impressions through the same bodily organ of sense; both without hesitation or doubt refer the sensation of sound to an external cause. But one has cultivated a sensibility to the simple sounds of nature, the other to the intricate and complex sounds of a refined art; and the result is almost as different as if each had been exercising a sense to which the other was a stranger.

For our next illustration we will take one which will lie closer to our subject.

Suppose now a man of science to be engrossed entirely by physical research. He spends his days of toil in the laboratory, in the observatory his nights of watching. Matter in its laws of combination, force in its various manifestations, are the exclusive objects of his meditations and inquiries. By these studies his faculty of observing physical phenomena, and detecting relations and differences between them, is sharpened to the highest degree; no angle of a crystal, no behaviour of a gas, no tremor of a suspended needle, no variation or perturbation of a star, no unusual line in a spectrum, escapes his notice, or fails to be brought under some general theory or law. But let us imagine him suddenly transferred from the familiar scene of his labours to a school of high art, where the recondite laws of beauty are discussed, and the relations which harmony of colour and grace of form bear to the æsthetic and moral perceptions are unfolded in trains of abstruse metaphysical reasoning. One can imagine him rubbing his

eyes as if he had awoke in cloud-land, and deem-
ing it a world of fantastic unreality into which
he had wandered; and perhaps it would be no
exaggeration to portray him as taking more
interest in the chemical structure of the paint
or the marble, than in the picture or the statue
on which others were gazing in a rapture of
admiration and delight.

Why, again, such an immense difference of
experience? Simply because the consciousness
of an external world, which is common to the
physical philosopher and the artist, has been
cultivated in very diverse directions; so that
where one mind perceives and comprehends,
another finds everything unintelligible and
unreal.

With these illustrations to guide our thought,
let us now return to the case which was propounded as a serious puzzle. Here are intelligent men, it is said, versed in science or
literature or active business, who experience no
difficulty in accepting and acting upon the
ordinary secular beliefs of mankind, but who
hesitate at theism, and regard it as an hypothesis which has but a vague and shadowy
foundation for its support. Whence this distinction, if all these beliefs depend alike on the
testimony of the human consciousness, and one

as much as another may be traced back to an instinctive inference from facts presented in it?

Simply, we reply, because with such persons the particular province of consciousness out of which theistic belief mainly springs is less cultivated, less developed, observed, and reflected on, than those provinces out of which the common secular beliefs arise. Of these beliefs the formative elements are distinctly present and familiar to most minds, and the results are proportionately clear and unquestioned. But the part of the consciousness which supplies the strongest evidence for belief in God is remoter from the world's ordinary life, more easily eludes analysis, and requires more of moral and spiritual culture for its development; and hence to persons immersed in worldly pursuits its witness is apt to appear inconclusive and untrustworthy.

Among no educated class of the community is a distrust of the argument for theism more rife at the present time, than among the rapidly-extending circle of the students of the physical sciences; and to their attitude towards it the explanation now given seems peculiarly applicable.

An exclusive addiction to physics forms in the mind a habit of closely scrutinizing and

reasoning upon facts observed by the senses,
and gradually invests such facts with a reality
which seems to be peculiar to them, and un-
shared by any other objects of human contemplation. Always dwelling on phenomena of
this sort, the mind is apt to lose its sensibility
to the more delicate and less definable actings
of the heart and spirit of man, and to acquire a
tendency to regard the more spiritual facts of
consciousness as dreams of the imagination,
the unsubstantial poetry and romance of
humanity. Even the more recondite laws and
conditions of Art come to be unappreciated,
much more the grandeur of the moral faculty
implanted in the breast of man, and the
yearnings of the awakened spirit after the
infinite and adorable Goodness. The consciousness thus becomes only partially developed; on
the side of sensible perception and logical induction it is abnormally quickened and active,
while on the side of the finer traits of humanity
and the spiritual sources of thought, emotion,
and desire, it lies uncultivated and dormant.

To such minds the theistic argument cannot
but be uncongenial. They demand solid facts,
such as can be examined, registered, measured,
handled, and rigorous induction each step of
which compels assent. Instead of these, the

argument for theism takes them back to the primitive elements of human consciousness, and precisely to those elements of it with which they are least familiar. Accordingly it seems to them fantastic, shadowy, inconclusive. That all their own science rests ultimately on nothing but the instinctive inferences of their consciousness they have long since forgotten, or if it is remembered it is only as a curious metaphysical paradox. Habit has inured them to the assumption that an external physical universe corresponding to their thought really exists; and from that basis they work on securely, oblivious that underneath all their results lies an hypothesis incapable of logical justification, and resting only on grounds of the same kind as those on which the despised argument for theism is based. Hence are engendered the partiality and injustice with which they draw a contrast in their thoughts between the logical certainty of science, and the speculative insecurity of belief in God.

We pass on now to consider a second difficulty, also of a logical character, which has been found in theism. It has been urged against the theistic conclusion, that it is infinitely larger than any which the premisses can possibly warrant.

P

The objection is put in this way. From any observed effect we have only a right to infer the existence of a cause adequate to produce it. If the effect is finite, our induction cannot lead to an infinite cause; only from an effect which we have previously ascertained to be infinite can an infinite cause be legitimately inferred. But the universe, if an effect at all, is so far as we know it a finite effect. Vast as it seems, it is not infinite, but infinitely less than infinite. If therefore we infer from it the existence of a Creator as its cause, it is only to a finite Creator that it can justly lead us. The power, wisdom, and goodness displayed by Him may transcend our experience in a degree which strikes our minds as unmeasurable; but between this vague immensity and absolute infinity there stretches an illimitable gap, across which our induction can never carry us to discover a really infinite Being. But a finite Being, however great, is not God, for of the God of our faith infinity in every attribute is an essential predicate; and therefore our induction from the universe can never lead us to God.

Such is the argument which is sometimes esteemed capable of demolishing theism. No doubt it is logically faultless, and if relevant would be fatal. Its one defect is that it does not touch the vital point; it misses the mark, and falls harmless to the ground.

Theism certainly does not rest on a scientific induction from the facts of the physical universe. If it did, no doubt all it could legitimately propound would be a primary physical cause sufficient to have originated the universe; and between such a cause and the living God the gap is indeed infinite. If the existence of a supreme Father be a truth, it is a truth not of science but of spiritual intuition. God is to be found, not at the end of a chain of logic or a series of phenomena, but in the depths of the human soul. From the contemplation of himself and of the universe, as interpreted by his own consciousness, man leaps instinctively to the belief in an infinitely powerful, wise, holy, and loving God, the Maker of heaven and earth, and the Father of mankind. This upspringing of the reasonable creature to its Creator, of the child to its Parent, is no affair of logic, and can no more be tied down to logical rules than the will can be bound by fetters of iron, or affection be regulated by mechanical action. Theism is the outcome of man's moral and spiritual nature, and can never be got rid of by logical refutation, but only by getting rid of all that is noblest and most divine in humanity itself.

The logical difficulties which are found in the theistic argument, however puzzling to some minds they may appear, have never probably exerted nearly as much deterrent influence as the moral difficulties which we have still to notice. These may be summed up in the mysterious existence of Evil.

There can be no doubt that when from the region of devout thought about God we bring down the idea of an infinitely mighty, wise, and loving Father into contact with the actual world around us, we are sensible of a surprise and a shock. Can such a world be truly His work? Do not its stern and sad realities contradict the intuition which discerns Him as its Author and Lord?

Alike to the philosopher contemplating the world from his study, and the philanthropist actively striving to alleviate its sorrows, the thought is apt to come unbidden, that if they had the task of constructing a world committed to them, nothing but want either of power or skill should prevent the exclusion from it of all waste and defect, all ugliness and incongruity, all decay, disease, and suffering, all physical and moral evil whatsoever. Perfect beauty, utility, goodness, happiness, would be their passionate aim, to realize which every faculty should be strained to the utmost, and no toil or pains be deemed too great a sacrifice.

We carry up this feeling into the presence of God, and are pained and perplexed. Apparently it has not been His feeling; and if not, how can He be the adorable Being before whose perfect goodness our souls have bowed down and worshipped? Or if He has felt thus, what becomes of His infinite greatness and wisdom? A God whose benevolent wishes can be baffled and thwarted is not the Being in whom we have placed our trust. "No God," is an intolerable thought, against which every holy and spiritual instinct of our souls rises up in unappeasable protest and rebellion. But neither in a God who is deficient in wisdom or power, nor in a God who is less than perfectly righteous and loving, can we find satisfaction and repose. The dilemma seems insoluble to our own intellect. Out of the depths of our humanity arises an irrepressible witness for a supreme and infinite Might and Wisdom and Love; but the world stands before us marred by imperfection, and writhing in the grasp of physical suffering and moral evil.

Before this awful mystery our speculative reason stands dumb and confounded. Yet we live, and on the whole are not unhappy. The evil which confronts us is not universal nor overwhelming. If the world is imperfect, it is nevertheless full of objects which gratify the senses and the appetites, minister to the desire for beauty in its various manifestations, and contribute in numberless ways to the welfare of mankind. If it abounds in suffering, it abounds immeasurably more in happiness. There is no organ created for pain, no natural instinct or desire which in its proper exercise is not an inlet of gratification and pleasure. If moral evil stains the face of society, and debases much of human nature, it is neither irresistible, nor irremediable in its consequences. No one need yield himself to be its slave, no one is debarred from shaking off its grasp by repentance and strenuous endeavour. Life with its sorrows and sins is found by the serious and sincere souls who follow Christ to be on the whole a beneficial discipline; and in devoting themselves to the service of truth, righteousness, and love, they experience joys for which a flawless world of ease and innocence would have afforded no occasion. Ask them how the dread mystery of evil has practically affected them ; and they will say that, in spite of everything which perplexes and pains them, they have felt the sense of a supreme Father's power and goodness penetrate and possess their hearts, with an intenseness and vividness all the greater for the trials through which it has accompanied them, and the burdens which it has enabled them to bear.

When, therefore, we set over against the evidence for theism the difficulty created by the mystery of evil, the effect is far from being overwhelming to our faith. To the practical reason of the believer in Christ, enlightened by his personal experience, it is not even serious. Utterly unable as he is to reconcile theoretically with the infinite perfections of the Creator the existence of such a mixed and imperfect world, he finds himself sustained in the midst of it by a divine Presence, and guided through its perils by a divine wisdom and love. Between him and his God the baffling enigma does not raise even a shadow of doubt. Who is he that he should comprehend all the ways of the Eternal? Evil may lie now like a ghastly incubus on the weary breast of humanity, but there is an eternal future in which the foul burden may be swallowed up and forgotten. In the meantime he can trust implicitly in the holy and loving One, to whom his inmost consciousness unceasingly bears witness. For that witness rises strong and clear within him, and never falters, notwithstanding the perplexing presence and pressure of evil. If the shadow of an inexplicable eclipse seems to lie athwart one portion of the universe, yet all the rest is still bright to him with the sunshine of heaven. If within himself he feels a sore struggle with weakness and sin, his soul only cries out the more for the divine Helper, and rejoices the more in the gift of strength and peace from above. And should he at any time of peculiar trial and weakness be bewildered with speculative questionings about the origin of the dark mystery, and his faith begin to waver under the impossibility of discovering a solution which can satisfy the intellectual faculty, he has only to retire within the sanctuary of his own heart to find God, and hear His voice, and feel himself cleansed and established by His gracious presence and fatherly consolation.

CHAPTER XI.

THE PHILOSOPHY OF THE PROOF OF THEISM, AND ITS BEARING ON RIVAL THEORIES OF THE UNIVERSE.

HAVING brought our argument to a conclusion, it only remains to offer some remarks on what may be called the philosophy of our justification of theism, and to point out its bearing on some of the theories about the universe which have been proposed as substitutes for the Christian belief in God.

Our basis is the veracity of the human consciousness, as the postulate which lies at the root of all human knowledge whatever.

Of each man's consciousness the primary and immediate object is himself. " I am " is the first element of reasoned knowledge. The conciousness of existence is prior even to the consciousness of thought. For, as it has often been pointed out, the famous formula, " I think, therefore I am," which makes existence an infer-

ence from the consciousness of thought, really
inverts the natural order. "I think" already
implies an "I," without which the formula
would be unmeaning.

"I am" is therefore the starting-point of
knowledge. But this primary consciousness of
self as existing is soon developed by reflection,
experience, and culture, into a considerable
body of knowledge about the nature of this self.
It is perceived to be something permanent, con-
tinuing the same through changes of sensation;
not merely a series of successive, unrelated acts
or impressions of the consciousness. Thus the
sense of personal identity is formed, and may be
called the earliest development of the primary
consciousness of existence. Then certain qualities of this permanent self are perceived. The
"I" is conscious of itself as thinking, and
exercising volition, and thus learns that it is an
intelligent and freely-willing agent. It also
finds itself distinguishing between right and
wrong, with feelings of approval and blame:
thus it becomes aware that it is a moral being.
Further, it is conscious of religious emotions, of
feelings and desires which reach out towards
the infinite, the unseen, and the eternal; thus it
completes its self-knowledge by adding spirituality to its other qualities.

By this unfolding of consciousness man comes to know himself as a person, endowed with will, mind, moral and spiritual affections.

So far the consciousness has evolved only the knowledge of self: we have now to observe its action in regard to that which is not self.

Man experiences many sensations every hour of his waking life, of which he finds it impossible to think that they originate in himself. By some imperative and uncontrollable instinct he refers them to external objects as their causes. However it may be explained, this is a universal fact of human nature, common alike to the savage and the philosopher. All believe, and cannot help believing, that the senses convey information of external things, and in their normal, healthy state may be trusted to convey the information correctly. Thus man becomes aware of a physical universe really existing all around him, and independent of him, and perceives it to be in permanent relation to himself. Then by classifying and reflecting upon the sensations which he ascribes to this cause, and interpreting them in the light of his own consciousness, he arrives at a conception of force and law, and of the universality of causation, and thus builds up the whole magnificent structure of the physical sciences.

It is manifest, then, that our knowledge of the physical universe ultimately rests on the veracity of consciousness. We get the facts in no other way than by an instinctive trust in our sensations to report correctly of an external world; and we make those facts into science by no other means than the instinctive application to them of conceptions which originate in our own consciousness. If we did not trust our sensations, the universe would be no more real to us than the dream of an uneasy slumber; if we did not transfer to Nature the sense of law and causation which we derive from our consciousness of will, it would be nothing but a succession of unrelated phenomena, and science would be impossible.

A physical universe governed by law is, however, not all that consciousness leads us to believe in, external to ourselves. The knowledge of other minds like our own, the minds of our fellow-men, is entirely due to it. In ourselves we feel mind, designing, purposing, and through the action of the will producing visible effects which are stamped with its impress. But we see similar effects around us which we did not ourselves produce; these we cannot but interpret in the light of our own experience, and we instinctively refer them to the agency of minds like our own. Thus our belief in the minds of other men rests on the consciousness of mind in ourselves; and were it not that we trust the inference to which that consciousness gives birth, we should have no knowledge of any human mind except our own.

But it is by no means at this point that the action of our consciousness finds its limit. When we have reflected on the efficiency of our own will to originate, and our own intelligence to purpose and design, we instinctively transfer the lesson of our personal experience to the realms of external Nature. Here, we say, are vast trains of phenomena, and the conviction takes hold of us that an efficient Will must have been at work to originate them. Here are arrangements, organisms, adaptations, which have all the marks of ordering and designing intelligence as known to us in ourselves; and again the conviction takes hold of us that a supreme Mind has been at work to design and construct them.

Nor is that all. Within our hearts we hear the authoritative voice of conscience, we perceive the eternal antagonism between right and wrong, we feel a solemn sense of responsibility; and this consciousness shapes itself instinctively into the conviction of a moral law laid upon

us, and a righteous Lawgiver to whom we are
responsible.   Once more, we are conscious also
of thoughts stretching away towards the infinite,
aspirations going up towards a supreme goodness, a craving to worship and trust; and out
of this consciousness grows a conviction, still
instinctive, of a supreme Father whose children
we are, and whose mercies are over all His works.

Such seems to be, in brief, the practical
working of the human consciousness.   By it
man is distinguished from the brute creation.
In its least cultivated state it witnesses to him
of his own personality and personal identity,
of the existence of his fellow-men and the
external world, and thus furnishes the basis on
which society rests.   Developed on the side of
will and intelligence, it gives birth to all the
arts and sciences.   Cultivated on its moral and
spiritual side, it leads to morality, religion,
theism.   These are its results, as it expands
under culture; and if civilized man, subduing
and interpreting Nature, beautifying his life by
Art, living righteously and unselfishly with his
fellow-men, and offering a grateful worship to
a supreme Father in heaven, is better than the
primitive savage of the wilds, then the instinctive assumptions of the consciousness, which
underlie the progress at every step, and with-

out which it would be impossible, may surely be said to be vindicated by experience.

Now our contention throughout the preceding discussion has been, that these several conclusions or verdicts of the consciousness are equally valid, and have their foundations, one as much as another, in the constitution of human nature. No one of them can justly be called more logical or more illogical than the rest. Whether we designate them intuitive perceptions, instinctive convictions, primary beliefs of the reason, or by any other name, they form one class, and in point of origin and in relation to proof are on a level. There is no rational ground for separating them into divisions according to their degrees of evidence, and calling some well-founded and others fantastic. Theism does not really stand at any disadvantage among them. It has vindicated its right to a place in their midst by an almost universal prevalence of its essential principle among mankind, a prevalence much wider than can be boasted by some at least of the scientific truths which are now allowed to be the most deeply rooted in the educated consciousness. It is not out of some single or obscure corner of the human consciousness that theism has sprung, but out of the most central region ; nor is it by any single voice that it is attested, but by the joint witness of the four grandest elements of our personality, namely, will, mind, morality, and spiritual aspiration. It is not a belief which is congenial to ignorance and barbarism, but dwindles and fades away with advancing civilization ; growing purer with culture it also grows clearer and stronger, and with every advance in true spiritual morality takes more thorough and entire possession of the heart. Nor can it be pronounced unprofitable or sterile in its actual working; its praise is written broadly on the whole story of human progress, and the most glorious triumphs of virtue have ever been inseparably connected with faith in the unseen God.

Hence if theism is to be rationally and consistently attacked, it seems that the attack must be made on the whole line of the beliefs which spring out of the general human consciousness, and not on theism by itself, as if it could be fairly singled out and separated from the rest. In other words, the attack must be based on principles which lead to universal scepticism. Deny the veracity and trustworthiness of consciousness, and knowledge and belief of every kind must perish in a common ruin. Strip man of his belief in himself, reduce him in his own estimation to an intermittent series of flashes of sensation ; and art, science, morals, religion, the universe, God, will all be blotted out by the veil of an impenetrable mist. Man must know himself to be man before he can know God. But the more thoroughly he realizes in his consciousness the wonderful and mysterious elements, intellectual, moral, and spiritual, of his own personality, the more will his adoring soul be filled with the glory of the supreme Father and Lord, in whom he lives and moves and has his being.

It remains for us to consider how this justification of theism bears on other theories which have been proposed as substitutes for belief in God.

It will doubtless have been noticed that throughout the discussion but a single issue has been raised. The choice has been represented as lying between agnosticism and theism ; that is, between complete ignorance about God, and faith in the living God. Not one of the rival theories, known as Materialism, Monism, Pantheism, Positivism, has been so much as named. And if the principle which animates the whole debate has been clearly apprehended, the reason of the limitation of it to this single issue will be apparent.

The principle is, that it is only through con-

Q

sciousness that man can obtain the knowledge of anything, whether in heaven or earth ; and hence it is through consciousness that God must be sought. If that method of seeking Him fails or is not valid, there is no other; we must abandon the search, and sit down in contented ignorance. This is the agnostic conclusion: God cannot be known ; man has no faculties capable of finding Him. But if, on the other hand, the method of consciousness is valid, and leads to God at all, it is to the living God that it leads, and to no other. For the inference is direct and immediate to the personal attributes of will, intelligence, righteousness, and goodness; if we arrive at anything at all, it is at these ; that is, at a God who wills, purposes, and is holy and loving; in other words, at a personal, living God. Had the method led us in the first place to the recognition of some self-existent Sub-stance, or first Cause, or primordial Force, or universal Tendency, or sovereign Principle of order; then a number of questions would have presented themselves for determination before we could have ascertained the nature of the result. We should have had to inquire whether this ultimate Entity was personal or impersonal, conscious or unconscious, an inherent property of matter, a Life or Soul pervading the world, a moral Agent, and so forth ; and in accordance with the answer would have been the resulting theory of the universe. But by following the method of consciousness all these debates are excluded ; there is no place left for them. It is the only method we know, and we stake all upon it. If it turns out to be invalid, we cannot know anything whatever about God; all we can put in His place is the absolutely " Unknowable" of the agnostic. But if it is valid, it leads us at once into the presence of the eternal Father, to worship, and trust, and give thanks. Theism or Agnosticism is therefore, we say, the only real question.

The way in which the rival theories are manufactured is full of instruction, when viewed in the light of the truth that all real knowledge comes to us through consciousness. The universe is first posited as a great objective fact, the logical faculty is then summoned to account for and explain it, and the resulting theory is according to the thinker's special turn of thought.

For instance, the student of physics observes matter shaping itself by occult laws, here into crystalline forms, there into vegetable organisms; here into living animals endowed with sensation and instinct, there into reasoning men. To his

Q 2

mind the several processes appear to melt insen-
sibly into each other, and to be undistinguishable
in kind, as if they were only various developments
of a single force or tendency; and as in none of
the results is he able to detect by the most
subtle physical analysis anything but the well-
ascertained elementary substances, he concludes
that all is matter, and only matter, although
it is possible that this universal material of
existence ought to be considered as something
superior to the inert, dead thing which popular
estimation reckons it.   Here, then, is full-
blown Materialism, accounting for life, mind,
conscience, religion, by the mere collocations
of material particles.

Another speculative mind, accepting the same
general theory of the universe, goes on to array
it in poetical hues, and gathers it up into a single dominant idea.   Unity here becomes the idol
of the imagination, which rejoices to see one in
all, and all in one.   Nature, however diverse
and manifold, is conceived of as an ultimate
Oneness.   Matter, force, life, mind, everything
whatever, are at bottom one, and are but Protean
shapes in which the One manifests itself.   Here
is an idealized Materialism, which has claimed
for itself the designation of Monism, the philosophy of Unity, of the One.

Another mind, again, starts from the opposite pole of thought, the ideal conception of the
Infinite. The infinite fills the mind, and leaves
no room in it for anything else. The infinite
is the All, and there can be nothing else; the
finite is unreal, inconceivable. The visible universe, then, must be the vesture of the infinite,
its transient manifestation, the shadow cast by
it, the phenomenal behind which the Absolute
conceals itself. Personality vanishes, for it
implies limitation, and nothing is real but the
infinite All. Here is metaphysical Pantheism,
in which human individuality is dissolved into
a phantasm.

For the commoner class of pantheists, however, so transcendental a theory is too unintelligible, and they adopt a simpler form of
pantheistic doctrine. From the notion of a
personal God they recoil, yet they feel unable
to banish mind from their idea of the universe. So they invent a compromise. The
physical Cosmos is conceived of by them as
a great organism, pervaded by a soul or life,
which is the principle of its coherence and
growth. This animating Principle manifests
itself in all the forces of nature, and all the
forms of sentient and rational existence. It is
life without consciousness, intelligence without

personality, a sort of infinite vitality transfused through the All. The rational element in man is but one of its manifestations, and hence men are denied any independent individuality, and are considered as merely localized portions of the one universal Life. Here is popular Pantheism, a system which has no very fixed or definite form, but varies from a vague poetical sort of theism at one extreme, to what is practically atheism at the other.

Now if the method, which we have called that of consciousness, be the only valid and trustworthy means of discovering the secret of the universe, it follows that these theories which are constructed by entirely different methods must be radically unsound. And their unsound-ness lies in this, that while they base them-selves, as in common with all human knowledge they cannot help doing, on the veracity of the human consciousness, they go on to deny the trustworthiness of its primary and fundamental testimony.

Look at the materializing theories. Their primary assumption is the existence of a material universe; the conclusion at which they arrive is that matter is all, and what is called mind or thought is nothing but a phenomenon caused by some special arrangement of its particles.

Well, whence did the framers of these theories get the existence of matter to start with? From the witness of their consciousness, is the only answer that can be given. There is no other means of being assured of the existence of an external, material world, than by trusting the universal instinct, which from the facts of sensation infers an objective cause of them in matter. These theories then rest, and must rest, ultimately on the veracity of the consciousness; that is the postulate, without which they cannot move a step. But, having borrowed this postulate, they build on it a proof that consciousness is not to be trusted, and speaks falsely in its first and most direct affirmation. For the primary consciousness is not of matter, but of mind, of the thinking personality within us. It is more certain to me that I am a personal mind or intelligence than that matter exists. Of my own thought and being I am directly conscious, but of matter only secondarily and by inference. If then I trust my consciousness in its testimony to a material world, much more ought I to trust it in its witness to my own personal mind. When, therefore, these materialists, after basing their theories on the existence of matter, argue from it to a denial of mind, they do in fact contradict the premiss from which their argument started. From the veracity of consciousness they deduce the illusiveness of consciousness; a course of reasoning which may be likened to a demonstration based on the axiom that if equals be taken from equals the remainders are equal, and leading to the conclusion that, after all, the remainders are unequal!

By a similar inconsistency the pantheistic theories are vitiated. They too cannot help relying on consciousness for their primary postulate, the existence of the universe which they seek to explain; yet they end in denying that individual personality to which each man's self bears witness as his inalienable possession. This, again, is to deduce the falsehood of consciousness from the assumption of its truth. Really, if a philosopher does not believe that he is an individual personal agent, he has no business to assume that there is any universe for him to frame theories about. And conversely, if on the witness of his consciousness he believes in the universe, it is absurd for him to set about proving that he himself is nothing more than a phenomenal shadow of the infinite, or an impersonal particle of the universal life. Pantheism and Materialism are alike self-contradictory, each overthrowing the foundation on which alone it can possibly rear its superstructure.

These considerations lead us to think that all such theories are too inconsistent in themselves, and too repugnant to the witness of the human consciousness, to be likely to maintain themselves as serious rivals of theism ; and that the real issue lies, as it has been already remarked, between agnosticism and theism; that is, between total ignorance about God, and belief in the personal, living God.

When at last we stand face to face with this issue, and have to make our choice, it might well be expected that nothing short of invincible necessity would induce us to take our stand on the blank, drear side of agnosticism, which explains nothing, promises nothing, holds out no succour or hope. But a system of thought has arisen, which undertakes to make our choice of agnosticism easy and delightful, and this accordingly claims a brief notice.

Positivism says to us, " Agnosticism is necessary and inevitable. About God nothing can be known. All the systems which human thought has devised to account for the universe, whether theistic, pantheistic, or atheistic, are a mere Babel of unmeaning words. On the side of heaven there is nothing for man but an absolute blank. But be of good cheer. Listen to me, and you shall not be without a Supreme Object to which your worship may ascend, and around which your holiest affections and dearest hopes may cluster with satisfaction and joy. Accept the religion of HUMANITY, and be happy."

We rub our eyes in amazement, and shake ourselves to see if we are awake. What! when our souls are crying out for an eternal, unchangeable, all-righteous, all-loving Father, to sustain them in their struggle, and satisfy their wants out of His inexhaustible treasuries of grace, is it possible that we can take up with the worship of poor, weak, imperfect, suffering human nature, and make that our God, and be content? Is not this to ask for bread, and be put off with a stone?

But Positivism has its explanations, and bids us not to be too hasty in our scorn of its offer. We are bidden to call the idealizing faculty into play. We are to think, not of individual men and women as we know them in our experience, but of the RACE. "Conceive of Humanity as a vast Whole," it is urged upon us. "Imagine it as a mighty Stream, of which all human beings, past, present, and to come, are the component drops; and see this majestic Flood emerging out of the bosom of the eternal Past, and ever swelling into grander proportions as it rolls onward to the unbounded Future. There is the true Supreme, the source of all goodness, the object of all worship, the sovereign ruler of destiny, the living force of the great drama of Evolution. What more can your souls desire?"

Wonderful juggle of words! is all we can answer. Man is melted down in the conjuror's crucible, and out comes a God! Positivism has stolen the properties of theism, and goes masquerading in them as if they were its own. The poor imposture provokes a sad smile, and we pass on with our spiritual thirst still unquenched, to prosecute our search for the living God.

Belief in a supreme heavenly Father on one side, on the other an absolute negation of all knowledge but that which is of the earth earthy; these are the alternatives between which the ultimate choice must be made. Let the honest waverer consider well what inducements each presents to persuade him to accept it.

Agnosticism claims to be strictly logical. The one point in its favour is, that it satisfies the faculty in us which weaves demonstrations and draws scientific conclusions. From that faculty it obtains against theism the verdict of "not proved." There its attractions end. It explains nothing; it satisfies no other faculty in our nature; it leaves the universe an inexplicable enigma; it leaves the human heart pining and empty. It has no significance but for the present moment; in the eternal future it finds a blank. If we accept it we must needs accept it under compulsion, as bankrupts accept ruin, and resign ourselves as we best can to inevitable destitution.

On the other side, the hypothesis of a heavenly Father offers the noblest satisfaction both to the reason and the affections. To our insatiable craving to know whence this magnificent universe with all its exquisite symmetry and beauty originated, it replies by pointing to a supreme Will and Mind, of which and by which are all these things. Of the deep mystery of our moral and spiritual constitution it suggests the only solution in which reason can repose, by revealing a supreme Righteousness which is mirrored in our consciences, and an infinite Goodness to which our restless aspirations ascend. Of all that is noblest in the development of humanity, it unveils an adequate cause in a divine Life from above breathed into human souls; and it alone accounts for that transcendent miracle in which the records of our race reach their culminating glory—the matchless and adorable character of Jesus Christ. The law of evolution in both the physical and moral worlds rests on it with security, as providing on the one hand the actuating force by which complex and multiform order and beauty have grown out of inorganic matter, and on the other the directing energy by which the course of providence " makes for righteousness." It sweeps away that hideous nightmare of despair, the thought that man with all his soaring aspirations and far-reaching desires has been made in vain; and by explaining his being, setting before him an aim worthy of his powers, and inspiring him with a hope high as heaven and large as eternity, it plants him on a rock in the broad sunshine of Truth, where he may labour and love and bear with patience, and work out his destiny in humble reliance on the supreme and perfect Goodness. Thus accepted by the reason, grasped by the affections, echoed back by the consciousness, verified by its practical working, the hypothesis of a supreme Father in heaven roots itself in the whole complex structure of the human personality, and makes luminous the otherwise inexplicable mystery of existence.

" Oh that I could believe it to be true !" the sincere doubter may still reply. " Attractive, cheering, satisfying, it no doubt is; but these qualities may belong to a dream. Proof my soul craves for; give me proof, and I will fall down and worship."

Well, there is one resource yet to be tried. Let the waverer put the hypothesis to the test by endeavouring to live and act as if it were true. He will thus discover in his own personal experience how it works. Let him interpret Nature, let him explain himself to his own mind, by its light. Let him live as if a holy Eye were ever upon him, a gracious Spirit ever at hand to cleanse and guide him. In the whispers of his conscience let him imagine that he hears the voice of the supreme Righteousness; in the unrest of his spirit let him try to think that he feels the upward drawing of the infinite Goodness. When passions are unruly, when duty is irksome, when temptations are strong, let him bring up before his thought the idea of an eternal Lord, whose name is Holy, to whom he is responsible and must give account. His joys and comforts and hopes, these let him at least provisionally associate with the conception of a Father's bountiful lovingkindness; his trials, his losses, his pains, with the thought of a Father's wise and profitable discipline. In a word, let him honestly and resolutely persevere in trying to arrive at a solution of the great problem by assuming theism to be true, and allowing it, at least for a time, undisputed rule over his life, both inward and outward in the world.

It is not for mortal and shortsighted man to predict anything with absolute assurance. But if the universal experience of sincere, wise, and beautiful souls may tell for so much as to warrant any prediction whatever, it is this, which accordingly in conclusion we venture to make. Let the trial be carried on in absolute good faith, with coherent and undiseased reason, and Belief in God will be the certain and inevitable result. No logical barrier will avail to keep it out. It will steal in at every inlet of the soul, insinuate itself with every lesson of experience, possess itself of every spring of thought and emotion, until the entire personality is filled and saturated with it, and the cry goes up to heaven, "My Father and my God!"

THE END.

Oxford
Printed by HORACE HART, Printer to the University

www.ingramcontent.com/pod-product-compliance
Lightning Source LLC
Chambersburg PA
CBHW020101030726
47498CB00006B/1892